JESS GLENNY

Ravelled Up

A journey into embodiment

First published by Embodied Press 2022

Copyright © 2022 by Jess Glenny

All rights reserved. No part of this publication may be reproduced, stored or transmitted in any form or by any means, electronic, mechanical, photocopying, recording, scanning, or otherwise without written permission from the publisher. It is illegal to copy this book, post it to a website, or distribute it by any other means without permission.

First edition

*This book was professionally typeset on Reedsy.
Find out more at reedsy.com*

Contents

Acknowledgement	iv
Praise for Ravelled Up	v
Foreword	vii
Introduction	ix
1 Autism	a flash of brightly coloured fish	1
2 Dance Movement	deep-water consciousness	23
3 Ashtanga Vinyasa	repeat and return	37
4 Hypermobility	tissue paper and glass	52
5 Teaching, Facilitating, Therapy	a womb, a limbeck	63
6 Writing	starburst and ocean	77
Afterword	93
Notes	94
Also by Jess Glenny	98

Acknowledgement

Thanks to Jane Belshaw, Norman Blair, Audrey Boss, Scott Johnson, Susanne Lahusen and Alex Svoboda for reading this book and writing enthusiastic recommendations, and to Theo Wildcroft for providing a Foreword so in sympathy with its tone and intention – this is exactly why I asked you!

Thanks to Jet Black for lending your artist's eye to various cover proofs, and to Elisabeth Heissler for creating such a beautiful cover.

Thanks to Las Autistas for reading and appreciating sections of this book when I was even more sure than I am now that no one would want to read it, and for being my Autista sistas.

Praise for Ravelled Up

"*A moving and intimate account of what the world of somatic practices looks like from the perspective of someone who is both Autistic and hypermobile. Jess writes with such mastery of words, poetics and imagery. Poignant, insightful and timely. I could not put it down!*" Alex Svoboda, PhD, founder of freedomDANCE

"*Jess takes the reader on an intimate journey into the experience of moving though life in an Autistic and hypermobile body. Thoughtful and thought-provoking, this book offers readers a tender and poetic glimpse – body, mind, heart and soul – into a life lived in a world that so often does not accommodate different ways of being.*" Audrey Boss, Food & Eating coach, Open Floor teacher

"*I feel privileged to have been offered a window into the world Jess inhabits as a dancer and an Autistic person, and as someone who experiences physical limitations and pain. As she says herself, she really believes in moving no matter what. Jess's words are a must-read for any student or teacher of movement who wants to understand some of what an inclusive movement space might need to incorporate.*" Jane Belshaw, 5Rhythms™ and Open Floor teacher

"Ravelled Up *is a work of beauty and raw honesty. Jess's words are prickly pears that refresh with their clarity.* Ravelled Up *has distinctly sharp edges; it jolts and judders the reader with forthright opinions and astonishingly beautiful writing. Jess does not fit in. She is just Jess. She writes: 'I pretend to go along with the mainstream view a lot more than I really do.' In this culture of intense commodification,* Ravelled Up *is invaluable. It will enhance your vocabulary, wake you up to other realities, unbalance you in remarkable ways."* Norman Blair, author of *Brightening Our Inner Skies: Yin and Yoga,* long-term yoga teacher

"I loved reading Jess's new book. Some thoughts and actions I could completely identify with, others felt remote from my own experience. None of this mattered. Her language is so rich and imaginative, her reflections created such a vivid picture of her life. Every page was a joy to immerse myself in." Susanne Lahusen, yoga and somatics teacher, Yoga Campus, London Contemporary Dance School

"Jess offers a beautiful meditation on her life, on what is really going on behind her eyes as a neurodivergent person. She shares deep insight into how she has seen and processed the world, at the same time offering the reader the opportunity to look more deeply into how they can find this insight in themselves. Importantly, this tender and powerful book leaves us with the opportunity to look again and again at ourselves and the people in our lives with compassion and understanding of whoever they are and whatever they are dealing with." Scott Johnson, director of Stillpoint Yoga London

Foreword

Jess and I have a very Autistic friendship – one without small talk or hanging out. The differences between us are as much of a delight as where we come together. And like Jess, I am in a phase of exquisitely sharp becoming. As I read this text (all in one sitting, in true Autistic fashion), I am poised on the brink of my third diagnosis, for an as yet unspecified auto-immune condition to add to the Autism and ADHD diagnoses of the past couple of years. I have been well and gently held through this process – in that I have been very lucky. And still, this process of self-recognition, of liberation, is terrifying and ecstatic in equal measure.

Unlike Jess, I do not know yet who I am becoming, nor how far back into my past I must travel to find myself. But like Jess, I have a compass and a stout staff to lean on. I hear the call of selkie and of fae, of the sea at the edge of the world, and the hidden roots of the forest. I will find my way without a map, through the call of the body, through cycles of movement and rest, of walking out and turning inwards.

I can't say if you, dear reader, will understand this book with the ease that comes from recognition. Herein lies a journey through fragments of memory that feels intimate and recognisable to me. I know the intensity of that inner world. Its joys and pleasures and associations are deeply familiar. I also had a recurring nightmare as a child, and I too understand the compulsion and the taboo involved in writing this kind of self – the false starts, the unpicking and the gathering, and the fear of repercussions.

Above all, I recognise the bravery in attempting to join these threads of neurology and practice, of dance and yoga, of writing and frozen speech into one text, one book.

Perhaps then, I can suggest how to read as you move forward – by letting the words flow and intoxicate, the images fill you up, and the threads knit together in their own time. Here you will find pieces of a collage – lines from fairy stories, moments of memories, literary citations, even mis-remembered metaphors. Recognise that neurodivergent people, stimming people, dancing and hyperlexic people, have learnt to recognise ourselves in the margins of culture, and hidden in plain sight.

To speak of this openly, as this book does, is an attempt to open a window onto both a way of living and a world of wonder. There is much that will feel alien here. There is no path that you can follow behind Jess to finish where she stands. I hope you can find it all the more marvellous for that.

Theo Wildcroft, PhD

Introduction

This is not a coherent narrative or a book of information. It's more like chinks that let in light on fragments of my life in movement as an Autistic person. Writing it, I often felt like a crazy lady. I'm still not convinced that anyone else wants to know about any of this. But somehow there was an impetus to set it all down. I wrote it for myself really, and readers are a bonus.

Some parts of this book are completely new. Other parts live an alternative life as articles on my blog. Over there, they may have somewhat different views and alternative vectors of travel. As I wrote this book, I was also making a rag rug. The process of doing over, repurposing, appeals to me. I am always weaving, morphing and changing. Print acts like a fixative, but the way you find these writings is really just a point in time. Everything is always in process.

There's also a lot of repetition. Echolalia ... refrains ... the things that come back to me again and again. I didn't try to edit too much of it out. Actually, I enjoyed the way that themes and thoughts and images recurred like waves, and I wrote them in. They represent the culture of my internal home.

Writing and movement have often been oppositional and conflicted for me. For many years, writing was my legitimate occupation, and dancing ... moving ... the life of the body ... was the mad woman in my attic – even though I danced every day.

What a relief it has been to understand that the dancer in me, the mover, is not separate and distinct from the writer, but that both emerge from a single ground of being and occupy the same space. No one needs to live in the attic ... or the cellar ... and neither has to do the work of the other. In this book, the writing is less a reflection on movement practice than a kind of co-arising, and it felt natural to include a chapter on the process of writing.

'Ravelling up' for me is a metaphor for the journey of embodiment: the process of knitting the random strands of myself into a useful garment. In this state of singularity, none of my experience of dancing, practising, teaching, writing and being a hypermobile Autistic person is separate and apart. Just as my experiences in these different but overlapping areas bleed into one another, so do the chapters of this book. If a piece is here when it seems to you it should be there, it probably could be in either location, but I have placed things where my felt sense tells me they ought to be.

A note on capital A and the language of Autism

Capital 'A' Autism is an indicator of pride. It signifies that Autistic people embrace Autism not as a series of deficits but as a cultural identity, a set of affinities that we share across our many individual differences. Where you see 'autism' and 'autistic' written with a lower-case 'a' in this book, I'm referring to autism as a diagnostic category, or as seen through the lens of neurotypical people who do not understand or embrace Autistic-originated understandings of Autistic identity.

In common with most #ActuallyAutistic people, I do not use person-first language ('person with autism') to refer to myself, because I see Autism as something that cannot be teased out and removed without taking the essence of me with it. I am an Autistic person, an Autistic.

I sometimes use the word 'Autist' to designate an Autistic person. I hear this word in various places in the Autistic community and am not sure where it comes from, but I didn't originate it.

'Allistic' describes a person who is not Autistic (or autistic).

1

Autism | a flash of brightly coloured fish

This chapter is about how movement practices, teaching, writing and Autism inform each other – how they spin from one distaff, and how they are constantly weaving in and out of each other to make a single fabric. While I was piecing this book together, I worried about whether readers would feel the connections between its parts. Would they discern the coherence I experience or would it seem random, a rag bag? Why does the Autistic experience belong intrinsically in a book about embodied movement? My friend Theo Wildcroft, Autist, yoga teacher, mover, postdoctoral researcher, explains it beautifully:

> We treat neurodivergence so often as if it is a mind problem or a brain problem, completely separated from history, bodies and relationship. A much more interesting story begins with the understanding that movement and sensation and thought are all part of the same thing. We learn to think through moving. We learn to move in response to sensation. And

> so neurodivergence is a sensory difference and a cognitive difference and a behavioural difference, because all of these things are part of the same thing.[1]

This chapter is about being Autistic, and it's also about being Autistic in an allistic world – the only experience of Autism any of us auti-folk has ever had. As the saying goes, 'If you've met one Autistic person ... you've met one Autistic person', so this chapter is not an Autism primer, more a few squiggled sketches of the experience of being Autistic as refracted through me.

Daleks

For as long as I can remember I have had a recurrent nightmare in which I am living under a violent occupation. Sometimes the ruling forces are Daleks, sometimes they're cinema Nazis, recently a middle-aged, 1950s-looking woman showed up from Gilead. The only way to survive in these nightmare regimes – at least for a short while, because discovery and death are inevitable in the end (that's the terrifying part) – is to appear utterly compliant, to blend so perfectly you disappear into the wallpaper. But the thing is, no one has really told me the rules, or maybe the rules just keep changing, and the *raison d'être* of a Dalek is EX-TER-MIN-ATE!

Autistic readers are probably one step ahead of me here, but for years and years I wondered about the origin of this nightmare. Then, as I turned fifty, I started to encounter the writing of Autistic people, began to recognise myself ... and you know the rest of the story. It's still shocking to me to realise that on the deepest level of my consciousness, I experience allistic culture as a cruel and ruthless totalitarian regime, in which any momentary lapse into transgressive (i.e. native Autistic) behaviour will almost certainly result in arrest and execution.

Autistic communities sometimes ponder why it is that from very early on in life, some of us become consummate maskers, able to pass (to the untutored eye, anyway) as allistic ... whereas others continue to behave in fabulously, flagrantly full-on Autistic ways. Perhaps one ingredient in the mix is our perception of the consequences of being seen to be Autistic. Now, you might say, 'But a Dalek is just a big old bakelite pepper pot on castors', but in the back of my mind, every time I commit an act of flagrancy (or perhaps I mean authenticity) – like advocacy, or coming out, or not suppressing a stim – I see that Dalek rolling in with its 1960s toilet plunger waving like a misplaced erection, and I feel as if I'm going to die.

I mask so well that sometimes I even fool myself, so my ADOS[2] scores were a bit of a shocker. It turns out that I'm more Autistic than even I had given myself credit for. ADOS aims to deconstruct that carefully composed micro-environment, the little bubble of breathable atmosphere that passing Autistics navigate the world in, like a goldfish in its bowl. ADOS prods and pokes. It hooks and pulls. It drags you way out of your comfort zone and inserts you into places you'd forgotten exist – where you always get fired, you don't talk to anyone at the party, and you fail again and again. And as horrible an experience as it was, I'm grateful to ADOS for shining a spotlight on that, because it affirmed for me how desperately I still struggle when you fish me out and demand that I breathe in air.

The most usual response when I come out to allistic people is incredulity. Often they seem confused, as if they're not sure what I mean or whether I'm joking. 'But you don't look Autistic,' they say. I'm not sure what they think an Autistic person looks like – or why they think this might be an appropriate comment to make. I *want* to look Autistic, because I *am* Autistic, and because Autistic people are my people. And despite masking I *do* look Autistic – to other Autistic people anyway.

I don't mask because I want to. I mask because most of my masking strategies are so old and so often repeated that they have become naturalised. I'd love to shuck them, but they're stuck in with little barbs. I'm like a person who left their native country when they were very young. 'Just be yourself', they tell me, my liberal and alternative friends. But I couldn't function in an allistic world unfiltered and unarmoured. I wouldn't be amusingly eccentric; I'd be something much more difficult and harder to accept.

Tripping off the tongue

I was drawn to words. Like a string of bunting they unfurled, and I wanted each brightly coloured triangle. I still do when I hear a language I don't understand. My mum always says that by the time I was a year old, she could have a conversation with me. I think she's exaggerating a bit, but I did learn to speak very early. At the same time, like many Autistic people, I also have verbal processing difficulties. I'm challenged by the phone, and I prefer to watch films with the subtitles on. It's a paradox, but I think that what's happening here has to do with hyperphantasia (thinking in pictures). I 'see' words and then have to translate them into meaning. This makes them rich, associative and freewheeling. It means that for me language is inherently poetic – elastic, suggestive, unfettered – and this opens up infinite possibilities for thinking laterally. But it also slows me down, and marshalling the images into parade-ground form takes energy, so processing language is also tiring. It's hard to make sense of words when they require me to do a specific thing, and especially when they require specific things in sequences (which plays into dyspraxia – a difficulty with orientation in time and space).

Autistic vocabulary is often noticeably different from the standard allistic lexicon. Our words of first resort may be ones that neurotypical people consider to be literary, archaic, academic or technical. I have an internalised self-judgement about speaking and writing this way, but Rachel, one of my Autistic friends, describes it as 'an authentic Autistic language'. I love that.

If there's a word that expresses precisely what I want to say, then I'm going to use it – and it doesn't matter to me if it's old or French or needs looking up in a dictionary. I don't try to conjure up arcane and poetic words; that's the way language comes to me. I do often try to dumb them down for conversation. It's as if there's a simultaneous translation app constantly running in my head, Autistic to demotic (on top, obviously, of the software that converts image to language). It's clearly one of those free ones that only gets two stars. In my autism diagnostic report, the assessor remarks that my speech is 'academic'. Even though I remember trying very hard to sound 'normal'.

This style of languaging gets interpreted in a variety of ways. Sometimes people tell me that I'm very articulate. I can see why they might think this, but actually, as I said, I have verbal processing difficulties. For me, words have a life of their own. They swim to the surface like a shoal of bright fish – and only a few beats later do I understand how each one pertains to meaning.

Isola

The physically, mentally and emotionally healthiest I've ever been (so far) was in 2020, the *annus mirabilis* of pandemic life. I realise, of course, that for many people 2020 was characterised by illness, loss, loneliness (or excessive proximity), financial ruin and more in that vein, but it really was *mirabilis* for me.

It's strange how an event that would have sounded to me, in 2019, utterly terrifying, actually turned out to be an interlude of something close to bliss. I guess disaster is actually often like this: selective and multifarious. I think about those people who lived their best life in the Blitz. But actually what I'm calling bliss is really just the circumstances to be well regulated most of the time – circumstances not ordinarily afforded to Autistic people in our culture.

Isolation, *isola*, island. In 2021, I'm bustled and jostled and wonder how to unpick the strands of last year and weave them in. I long for sanctuary, for the Skellig of my inner world, to abandon the pots and kettles for the asylum of the sea. I want to make it simple again and spacious. I want to feel crisp at the edges, differentiated.

There's a goose on Southmere Lake with angel wing. I wonder what it's like for that goose when the flock lifts off and arrows north. I would like to be that goose. I would like the aloneness and the empty lake, the gaggling voices fading, and the way the world clarifies, revealing a thin line, a boundary between me and it.

Passing

I want to ... I'm relieved when I do – I won't be sent to a gas chamber or exterminated by Daleks ... but I'm also disappointed. I feel unseen, unmet, misapprehended. You see, I am not one of you. You see, when I am absolved of the horror of difference I am also relieved of my culture and identity.

It starts when you're very young. When you realise they will not let you be a selkie, and you have to crawl out of your skin. You do not know that they will hide it under a stone and it will take nearly fifty years to find it again. You do not know that in the meantime you will sicken and starve and wall yourself up in a castle. You do not know that you will cross the drawbridge and re-enter the world like a hungry ghost, a vortex that cannot stop spinning.

Even when you find your skin, you cannot just slip into it any more. You know too much about tea-cups and spoons, aprons and flowers. Neurotypical-mimicking ways are like ivy. The tendrils bind into your bones.

I'm like a person who left her homeland as a little child and learnt a whole new way of life, but deep inside still moves to the beat of the old country. Or as an Autistic friend of mine put it, it's like being an undercover detective. In the end, the two lives become so ravelled up, you hardly know which one belongs to you any more.

Xanadu

Looking back, it's clear to me that Mrs Burton was Autistic. But this was 1972 and we didn't yet have a word for ourselves. We didn't have an ourselves. Mrs Burton lived in a bungalow in

Gudgeheath Lane. The garden was overgrown and full of rescue animals. The year before I was in her class, Mrs Burton rescued a lamb and somehow managed to keep it in the school field. This was long before OFSTED[3] was thought of, and the notion of a standardised primary school curriculum was still dystopian. Once, for a few experimental weeks, our headteacher instituted the Summerhill system[4] and we chose which lessons to go to. The lamb was called Larry.

Mrs Burton lived in an amorphous middle-ground of age. She wasn't young, but she wasn't old. In hindsight, I guess she might have been in her early forties. She wore shapeless tweedy skirts that finished just below the knee, loose blouses with blouson necks and floppy ties, the ubiquitous 1970s tea-coloured tights, and flat shoes. Her dark, straight hair looped over her ears and around the back in a shambolic Victorian bun. I remember her with dog-brown eyes – sharp but not unkind. However, I may have made that up.

I didn't especially love, or even like, Mrs Burton. What's remarkable about the year I spent in her class is that for the first time in my school life (I was nine), I felt comfortable. It's hard to convey how extraordinary and unfamiliar an experience that was. I didn't give much thought to it at the time, only I remember once trying to explain it to my mum. It came out much smaller than it felt, and I could tell she was puzzled. I described it, I think, as being at home in Mrs Burton's class, feeling that I belonged. I understand now that this was because in subtle, silent, unspecifiable ways, Mrs Burton's classroom was Autistic space. She didn't try to make it that way. Inclusivity hadn't been invented yet. *It* was because *she* was.

I still remember the geography of the tables in Mrs Burton's classroom. They were anchored like continents in a stable and unshifting world. I sat at a long one – two tables placed end to end – near Mrs Burton's desk. I was on the desk-ward side, and there was a window several chairs down to my left. I moved to another, big square, table to learn about evolution – fish crawled out of the swamp onto a land forested with enormous primeval trees; stegosaurus gave way to brontosaurus, to tyrannosaurus rex; proto-people crept out of the undergrowth with stones. There was a new and thrilling cassette-tape episode every week.

We must have done maths with Mrs Burton I suppose, but I don't remember any. In my memory the classroom thinned and cleared repeatedly around pools of imaginary space. Mrs Burton read us magical books like *The Weirdstone of Brisingamen* and *The Wizard of Oz*. She read us Coleridge's opium-inspired 'Kubla Khan', probably not generally considered an appropriate poem for nine-year-olds, but I loved it.

> In Xanadu did Kubla Khan
> A stately pleasure-dome decree:
> Where Alph, the sacred river, ran
> Through caverns measureless to man
> Down to a sunless sea.

I didn't completely understand the words, but I absorbed the music of the language, and I intuited meanings that underlay the literal ones. 'Kubla Khan' still loops through my head from time to time.

It's hard, it seems, for allistic people to understand how – and how much – Autistic people are excluded. This is, in my experience, particularly evident in the prone-to-spiritual-bypassy worlds of yoga and conscious dance. Serendipitously, while I was writing this piece, I came across the work of disability activist Mia Mingus. Mia blew my mind. She had not just words, but well-formed thoughts and cogent sentences for something I had dimly sensed, experienced constantly, but never been able to knead out of flour and water into the useful consistency of dough. Mia coined the phrase 'access intimacy'. She says:

> Access intimacy is that elusive, hard to describe feeling when someone else 'gets' your access needs. The kind of eerie comfort that your disabled self feels with someone on a purely access level. Sometimes it can happen with complete strangers, disabled or not, or sometimes it can be built over years. It could also be the way your body relaxes and opens up with someone when all your access needs are being met. It is not dependent on someone having a political understanding of disability, ableism or access. Some of the people I have experienced the deepest access intimacy with (especially able-bodied people) have had no education or exposure to a political understanding of disability.[5]

In Mrs Burton's class, I experienced access intimacy.

In 2021, school regulation makes it difficult for an Autistic teacher to survive, never mind thrive. Our genius is left-field, doing it differently. We don't / can't / why would we want to stick to the manual? Autistic children in the UK can now be diagnosed and statemented, and should, in theory anyway, receive specialised help to negotiate school, but they're unlikely to experience the kind of truly Autistic space I lucked into in Mrs Burton's class.

This is not just a celebration of a single teacher, but a paeon to the whole awkward, eccentric tribe of us who didn't bother to read the instruction book and are spinning it out of our own bodies like spider web. The best Autistic spaces are strange, capacious, ingenious places where it's safe to be. They inspire. They contain but they don't constrain. They're vast in their scope and particular in their attention to detail.

Mrs Burton loved words and, being (I believe) Autistic, could get a bit pedantic about them. She told us when we wrote a letter we should never contract our county name to the awful 'Hants' but should allow it the full expansion of 'Hampshire'. I think she'd like that I write. I hope she'd be pleased that I'm writing about her, but I think she'd be a bit embarrassed.

Georgia O'Keeffe at Ghost Ranch

Georgia's room is empty but for some curves: what look like enormous shells, and a painting of a swerve; a prickly plant; work things; plain, monastic walls; and a long rectangle of desert.

I long to be in Georgia's room. I long for that concentration within the landscape sweep. I long for the solitude and silence, and for that singularity, the hardening into edges, identity forming, the sense of a discrete self that isn't constantly being eroded against the corners of irrelevant things.

Just lately, I've fantasised about a t-shirt that says, 'Everybody Fuck Off'. I've wondered how I could really be an anchorite – the practicalities of it. I feel *cabined, cribbed, confined, bound in* by everything human that inserts its fingers: people with their opinions and projections and relational needs. I feel like Ariel stuck in a tree, or maybe more like Sycorax who stuck him there in a moment of terminal irritation. *The isle is full of noises.* All of them too loud.

This desert with it's mid-ground feathering of trees, hot scumbled mountains, big skies, looks vast and empty, scoured of everything that isn't necessary. And Georgia, in profile, black against the sun, is absorbed and starkly alone.

I guess it's an illusion. Someone must have been behind the camera. I don't like to think of that. The other one misarranging all the things and wanting dinner.

I will make it happen, though. The desire is too clear and strong not to manifest itself, clean like a bone, incisive. The door closes. The room is still and cool. The clamour falls away.

Garage witch

I always wanted to be a witch. A witch is unto herself. Her edges aren't always drizzling into this and that like a poorly executed watercolour. She lives in a world of mystery, and she also lives in this world here and now, bright and intensely coloured, plying this world's things – buttons, string, salt and leaves – maker of salves and poppets. She's a solitary and a weaver of webs. Her significant other is a cat.

The garage was up the back-garden path, facing the back-door out of the kitchen, and it had its own door on a latch. It had hanging lamps and tins and mysterious instruments, glue and things that smelt of petrol, benches and dusty hessian sacks. It was a witch's house, a place to hole up and make a potion out of petals and leaves.

I loved Carabosse in the fairytale book, curved like a cartwheel and attended by a retinue of spiders and rats, and beetles with shiny carapaces. Witches don't care what they look like; this unhitches them from social reinforcement, gives them power. They don't need your approbation, and that makes people scared.

Witches live on the peripheries and they also don't care about that.

I wonder why they didn't invite Carabosse. Perhaps they didn't like her. Perhaps she was too direct. Perhaps they didn't appreciate her hanging out with spiders, or her clothes weren't right. She probably didn't want to go anyway, but when the invitation didn't come, she had to make a show of it – otherwise you're just the one who's disregarded, not the one they fear.

I liked drawing Cinderella's gowns, the colours and lines, but I never wanted to be her. I didn't want the palace or the boring prince. Sycorax, 'a witch ... so strong / That could control the moon, make flows and ebbs'[6] but still residing on the edges of the text ... Dog lady Hecate ... Baba Yaga in her house of bones ... These are my people, the ones with roots and meanings, presiding over limens, self-possessed. I feel them surging through me like a pack of wolves howling their place on this Earth.

It is not the words

Judith Scott was an artist (she died in 2005). She made large, intricate, colourful pieces by wrapping with yarn and strips of cloth. Inside these womb-like, containing spaces, x-rays reveal concealed objects: forks, rings – small daily items from her immediate environment. Judith also had Downs Syndrome; she was D/deaf and non-speaking and spent her life up to the age of 43 in institutions. Here, when she was a child, crayons were taken away from her because she was considered too 'retarded' to be able to use them – even though she clearly *was* using them, perhaps not in the way the staff expected, but artists do the unexpected with their materials. Judith's medical notes record that after the crayons were taken away, she cried for hours.

The introduction to a video about Judith on Karmatube[7] poses the question, 'Can something be called art if it is made by someone who does not consider herself an artist?' I wonder why it's assumed that Judith didn't consider herself an artist. Because she didn't speak, write or sign? Because she didn't articulate artist as a word? Is the word required to make what's happening real? Folded into the assumption that Judith did not consider herself an artist is a second one that because she didn't speak, write or sign, she didn't reflect. But as soon as she got the opportunity, Judith spent every day, all day, making art, continuing sometimes until her fingers bled. It seems to me that her work is a body of non-verbal reflection and that she communicated her identity loud and clear.

Like many (but not all) Autistic people, I think in images and translate into words. My thought-pictures are evocative, textured and intensely compelling. I also experience emotion as image and similarly have to slowly deduce – or maybe it's more like seduce – the terminology for the feeling from the colours, lines, tone and content. It's a kind of internal pathetic fallacy. For some visual thinkers, see-thinking is realistic. Temple Grandin, animal behaviour scientist and grandmother of the Autistic self-advocacy movement, explains that her visual memories are like computer files stored in her brain.[8] They are accurate and precise and make her a highly skilled structural designer. This way of thinking enabled her to note design faults in the Fukushima nuclear plant and predict the disaster that occurred there as a result of the tsunami in 2011.[9] For me, though, see-thinking is mythopoeic. It's an art house movie, an expanding, interconnecting sequence of images that carry meanings on multiple levels, psychological, emotional, somatic.

It was only very recently that I realised most other people's mental processes don't happen this way, and I'm still puzzled by how it's possible to think without seeing it. It turns out to be equally difficult to convey to non-see-thinkers what it's like to see-think and how the translation process works. For a start — in my mind anyway — there are always many layers of interpenetrating images going on at the same time. 'Going on' because they're not static like paintings; they shift and change, and I can move between, into and through them. I can also alter them, though where this 'I' is located, what is volitional and what arises organically beyond 'my' control, is not entirely clear to me. I suppose it's really a dialogue of unconscious and conscious mind. Once I start to transpose image into word, the words themselves arise as image — sometimes typed in Courier on a strip of paper — and then generate more images, so meaning is rich and multi-dimensional — often overwhelmingly so.

In the process of paring and refining into language, much of the expansiveness, beauty and subtlety of the original vision gets lost frustratingly in the gaps between the words. And there are experiences and feelings that simply have no words in the English language, or for which language fails to provide fine enough distinctions. It's like a fishing net: the holes are always bigger than the string:

> When the phone stopped ringing she perceived a peculiar silence. One of many. Which one? There is a silence of perception. It wasn't that. Thoughtless silence? Forced silence? Chosen silence? Silence because you're listening. Fearful silence. Because the radio's broken. Hesitation. When you don't say it because you don't want to hurt the other person.

> Enraged silence. When you don't say it because it's not going to do any good. Waiting. Thinking. Not wanting to be misunderstood. Refusing to participate. Self-absorption. When a loud sound is over. Shame.[10]

I wouldn't be surprised if someone like Judith Scott found verbal language just too much of a dispersal of creative energy. I'm not D/deaf and I find it exhausting. I'm hyperlexic, meaning that I have a significantly higher than average ability to understand the written word, coupled with a much smaller ability to understand spoken language. My intuitive sense is that I read body language and facial expression preferentially; I definitely find speech harder to process when these are not available, and I detest the phone. My hyperlexia seems to me a paradox. I feel that it arises out of the secondariness for me of word as a mental process and a sense of the urgency of translation if I am to swim in the shoal. Because no one wants to be eaten by a shark. Yet I write seldom. It's too arduous; the sense of the breadth of the of the gulf to be bridged too daunting. While in a sort of way words allow me to feel connected, they also fix me in isolation – because words are cyphers, and the actual experience always floats silently between them just out of reach. As Hamlet says, 'My words fly up, my thoughts remain below.'[11]

It's said that 70 per cent of interpersonal communication actually occurs not through the clipping of words but through the body, so perhaps hyperlexics are actually more tuned in than the average person to the full range of human expression and are in fact listening where it really counts. And it cuts both ways. My hands are very articulate. I speak with them a lot. They often carry meanings from inside that I haven't yet been able to understand intellectually or that words lack the subtlety and finesse to encode. When I began to investigate the possibility that I might be Autistic, I learnt that body-speaking is a defining ability of Autistic people. There's a term for it. The term is 'flapping'. Yes, 'flapping' ... as in penguin. Many Autistic people who have been in special education aimed at training them to pass – to appear as seamlessly neurotypical as possible – recall the instruction, 'Quiet hands!', meaning that they should sit on it and shut up. God forbid you should get the crayons if you don't know how to use them![12]

It's no news to anyone, I think, that in our culture the mind is prioritised and privileged, while the body and its productions are denigrated. Whereas in earlier times the suppression of the body took the form of a kind of moral demonisation – even furniture had to be clad in tablecloths and antimacassars in case it got too exciting – today the body is commodified on an industrial scale. Even loci of somatic enquiry and embodiment, the holy asylums of the speaking body, have been infiltrated and commercialised. Who would have thought we could be brainwashed into buying 'improved' versions of our own bodies? No wonder so much energy goes into silencing the Autistic body. A body that speaks irrepressibly its own meaning has the potential for very exciting subversion.

I found out about Judith Scott from Emma Roberts. Emma is a 5Rhythms™ dance teacher and a fellow explorer in the badlands of the moving body. As a child, Emma was told she had 'ants in her pants and poor concentration'.[13] But what if she was concentrating on the ants in her pants? After all, she went on to train in classical dance, which requires a great deal of focus – and a lot of ants. What if the ants in her pants were the way she was communicating? What if she was just speaking her primary language?

As an Autistic person, I'm likely to give you the wrong change and the wrong date, my short-term memory would shame a goldfish, and I don't know left from right or the difficult bits of the times tables, but I do have a first-class degree and a doctorate (in Pictures and Words, of course). As someone with Ehlers-Danlos, I struggle to stand static, and have to do a huge amount of daily conditioning work to be able to sit unsupported for more than a couple of minutes, but in my late fifties I have an ashtanga practice that would be beyond many people in their twenties. Both Autism and hypermobility involve binaries of deficit and hyper-ability. It feels dishonest to describe myself as disabled, and dishonest to describe myself as not disabled. I live in a floating space of both / and, neither / nor. Judith Scott's deficits appear far more evident, and yet they bleed so seamlessly into her genius as an artist. It seems incontrovertible to me really only that Judith Scott was Judith Scott.

Can you see the music?

One of the moments that has stayed with me from my lovely, woo-woo early-1970s education is being asked to listen to a piece of classical music and write a creative response. As so often in my childhood when a task appeared to have no set parameters or these were not explained, I was overwhelmed by the breadth and scope of the task in hand. Nowadays, I would extrapolate, refine a theme and mood, but then I felt as if I was meant to be writing down everything I could see, and the extent of that was *ginormous.*

I receive music through my ears like everyone else, but what happens when it enters the sorting house of my brain appears to be a little different. I see music in two ways at the same time.

First, there's the stream of images – the art house movie – and then there's something more literal that happens inside my physical head and which I can watch. It could be coloured balls bouncing, laser lights arc-ing, grey lines hatching and re-hatching, that kind of thing. There's an infinite number of possibilities. Seeing music in this particular way (rather than, for example, tasting it) is called *chromaesthesia*.

When people learn that I see music, they're often amazed. They think that seeing music must be very cool. In a way, it is, but it's also perfectly ordinary – just as seeing the physical world is both perfectly ordinary to a sighted person, and at the same time the most extraordinary thing.

I wonder what it would be like to hear music cleanly, without the patterns and colours – overlaid on the art house movie. I try to imagine that. Perhaps it would be a kind of mathematical purity (imaginary of course; in reality, maths lives behind a 'no entry' sign for me). Perhaps it would be a clear stream ... or fine and angelic with the contours of those long medieval trumpets and flowing robes. But, darn, I'm seeing all of this. I think there would be a simplicity, even a sense of relief perhaps. I think that maybe things would slow down and clarify into one thing: a tumbling current of non-transmutable sound. It certainly would be different.

Patti Smith Riff

M Train[14] is a book about nothing – about the in-between spaces, the wadding of human life. Patti makes the crevices feel fertile and itchy with green, a 'nothing' like rich, dark, velvety boxes lined with stuff. Patti makes it permissible to expend days in wandering / wondering at random, musing, writing, and sitting too long at off-times in cafes. She makes it possible that this is itself a life.

Sometimes, serendipitously, Patti meets a strange personal idol. She seems to have no sense that she is herself a famous person and that her idols are probably awe-struck and delighted to meet her.

I wonder if Patti is one of *us*.[15] Her father spent many years devising a handicapping system for horses, but he never placed a bet. He had 'a mathematical curiosity ... searching for patterns'. He was 'kind and open-minded' but 'dreamily estranged'. Hiroshima and Nagasaki 'broke his heart'. 'Question everything', he told his children. He always wore the same thing: 'a black sweatshirt, worn dark pants rolled up to his calves' (surely an Autistic touch) 'and moccasins'. At the weekend, the children were 'obliged to give him some privacy as he had little time for himself'.

Patti talks to inanimate objects, which have personalities and a view. She spends days roaming around on her own, coming upon people, places and things. Patti is obsessive – she says so herself. I think perhaps rather, though, she is immersive. She immerses into worlds – of books and lives and TV programmes – like blotting paper sopping into a dish of ink. She is herself an immersive world. A mood. A music. A dish of ink.

I first became aware of Patti in in 1978: 'Because the Night' and the iconic cover of *Easter*. I was fifteen. She was upraised arms, white camisole, and flagrant dark armpit hair. She embodied something I couldn't define and didn't understand, but wanted inchoately. I've always adored armpits with their soft, tender hair – the shape, the undulations and hollows, the suggestion of hidden places and sex. Patti didn't conceal hers or do the polite thing and depilate. She flaunted them, these beautiful, unseemly, ordinary things. I was slow. It took a long time for the penny to drop. I had lovers who were men, and I liked their silky armpits. At some point, eventually, it occurred to me that I could have my own – farouche and fuck-you and normal – and ever after, I did.

I wrote this in the wrong book, at the back of the Mysore class register. It arose in the interstices – a weed on a page not intended to cultivate actual writing. I wrote it in Patti space, drifting an hour or so, in the Greenwich Picturehouse downstairs, cake for breakfast, rain drilling the tarmac, slick olive trees, St Alfege's, massed and matronly, presiding. It's not a list of names and payments, but it's hiding out here like an outlaw, whisky-toting, red kerchief, hooves on rocks.

Anthropomorphic

I've just read *Piranesi*.[16] It struck me as a rather Autistic book in all sorts of ways. One of them is the relationship between Piranesi and his inundated world, the House. Piranesi communicates with aspects of the environment that would not ordinarily be considered capable of talking back, including the House itself. What's in the House, we are told, is all that has been exiled from the modern world; however, communicating with non-sensate things has never been exiled from the Autistic universe.

As an Autistic person, I cannot help but feel that everything is alive. This sounds quite nice, but actually it's fraught with existential difficulties and a sense of ongoing distress. It's excruciatingly painful to throw away an object when I think the thing will feel rejected, or worse that I'm killing it. Then there's eating stuff. I cannot bite into a Jelly Baby or a Pom

Bear or a meringue that looks like a duck. And I've never forgotten Tommy the Tomato from schools TV, who screamed when he was about to be cut up. I've no recollection of what the programme hoped to educate me about (fractions probably), but my heart still twists when I remember the terror of Tommy before the knife. Of course, I know rationally that Tommy was an animation, and a worn-out sock is not a sentient being, but the force of feeling always carries off the voice of reason.

At the heart of it all I think there's a kind of Autistic atavism. For most of human history, everything was made of something that was once alive, and we knew what those things were and where they grew, fed or roamed. We were in bio-relationship with every object we could ever encounter or possess. Now the origins of things are remote and mysterious, but for me the sense of relatedness remains. We are still stuff of a single universe, dust of the same combusting stars.

I'm pining for a more traceable kind of bio-relationship – one made out of wood and wool and thatch. I want a broom, not a robot Hoover. I want to feel low to the ground and close to the roots of things. I want to kill cleanly and use materials well. There's no respectful way to relate to a plastic yoghurt pot that that serves its purpose for a couple of weeks and takes millennia to biodegrade. We live in an age of terminal decadence.

For Piranesi, the House is a place of beauty and wonder. He studies its tides, and maps the songlines of its halls. In its dreaming time he forgets the dystopian universe he was snatched away from. For me, the House feels oddly like Autspace. I, too, was seduced. And when Piranesi travelled back through the portal in the Hall of Fauns into the world with petrol fumes and more than seventy people, I also felt a sense of loss.

2

Dance Movement | deep-water consciousness

This chapter is about dance as a somatic practice. It's about receiving movement from impulses within rather than reproducing choreographies; about offering witness to inner experience rather than creating smooth aesthetic surfaces. These are dances that don't come pre-formed or notated, and they are never revised or reproduced. They exist on the wing and dissolve in the moment.

I could have called this chapter 'conscious dance', but actually, my somatic dance practice has been a bit wider than that, and anyway, the 'conscious dance' moniker has never really jibed with me. It seems to me that what's fundamental about this way of dancing is that it enables us to access what is *not* yet conscious. And then, at the same time, what would *un*conscious dance look like? Operating theatre? Zombie horror? Really, I think, in this kind of movement practice we are standing on the edge of consciousness, looking into a pit of darkness, with curiosity and a willingness simply to receive (as best we can) what rises up – bubbles, vapours, smoke, volcanic eruption, or nothing much.

Alex Svoboda, a Russian friend and colleague, tells me that the Russian term for what we do translates as 'spontaneous dance'. I like that quite a lot. The Latin root *spons* encompasses meanings such as 'impulse' and 'motion', and Merriam-Webster defines *spontaneous* as:

> : proceeding from natural feeling or native tendency without external constraint
> : arising from a momentary impulse

Native, impulsive, unconstrained in motion. The latch lifts, the hatch drops open, we fall, float, glide into this current of consciousness, the place that's always waiting, a native country, a dreaming space, like coming home to this moment.

A dancing life

I think I have always been a dancer. The earliest dance memory I can date is from 1968, when I was five. *Top of the Pops* is on TV, and it's me and Mary Hopkin, dancing forever and a day. That was the life we'd choose all right.

I've told this story before, so it seems a bit fossilised – caught in time – in a way that I slightly distrust, but I do remember my five-year-old passion for this song, and being moved by dancing to it into a place beyond some kind of threshold. And I also remember doubting whether this was a place I was allowed to be. I think now that this 'beyond' lay outside the careful city of Autism Masking, where to blend is to continue to be alive. All the dystopias – fictional, historical, geographical, or located in gender or race – have this in common.

I've felt like a selkie for a long, long time but only in fairly recent years have I received the tools (Autistic identity, community and diagnosis) to understand that for me fundamentally the selkie is an Autistic person trapped in a allistic world. The sea is the place of my people: boundless, fluid, liberating, embracing – it even supports our hypermobile bodies with a density of gravity through it's watery skin. But there's a strong pull from the house. The selkie chooses (albeit without having read the small print) to live on land. And in the process of bearing and raising a child, she becomes almost naturalised – but not really. There is always this sense of dys-location and longing for return ... and also the teacups, apron, the kettle and saucepans, the hollyhocks and the earthenware pots – land things that she can no longer simply shuck off. So she teeters in-between, washed up on land, drowning in air and straining for the release of the sea.

Greylands

It's both easy and difficult to move from underwater consciousness. When I'm there, it feels effortless, like riding a slipstream, but actually the cognitive brain is always exerting a counter-force. Being 'in' the dance takes the discipline of one thousand moments when you quietly insist on return. It isn't enough simply to wait. Your dance may come to you now and then, but that isn't a practice. On the other hand, you cannot take it by force. You have to wait out in the bushes and creep silently, with an end in mind and yet without intent, as if being in the bushes were the sum total of your expectation, and then it may come, like a rush of birds rising out of the trees.

Still, there are times – many of them – when only the greylands are there: vast, empty, woolly and hard to breathe, like some endless mental tundra. I hate the tundra; it scares me with its size and colourlessness and enveloping atmosphere. Every dancer knows the tundra: 'I couldn't get into it today.' So then there is a call to attention to this too – even this: not running or turning away – never do that – not whistling for the wolves, because they will not come. Just holding ground and listening for anything – the crack of a stick – something small and insignificant that can hook you and pull you up, up and out.

Swinging out across time

5Rhythms™ wasn't my first formal dance movement practice, but it's the one I grew up in (so to speak), danced most regularly and for the longest. Before 5Rhythms™, I couldn't string myself out over time; I couldn't abseil from moment to moment. This manifested in a lot of ways, but an obvious one (to me) was that I couldn't stand up in front of people and talk. I couldn't freewheel a lecture or spin out a class on the wing. Dancing the Rhythms taught me to emerge what comes next – whereas before, I structured myself on a grid of rules: a table of time.

I think this table is still helpful as a template – a ground to spring off or abandon entirely for a while. It can become overgrown with grass and wild flowers so you have to parse the undergrowth to find the metal. (I know that this is not what 'parse' *means*, but it's what it feels like – the texture in my thumbs – and what we are doing, really, as we spread the words and the parts of words, the fine black filaments on the white ground, and sift carefully with our fingertips for meaning.)

This liquification of time changed my life. It turned me from a selkie living in a house who had forgotten about her skin ... into a selkie who remembered. I don't think we are ever free of the iron teeth of the house attached to our ankle actually. But knowing the sea – having access to its wild processional of waves – that changed everything. The difference was that I knew I was born to swim.

When I started dancing 5Rhythms™, I'd already been practising yoga and doing ballet and other technique dance classes regularly for many years. It wasn't moving *per se* that liquified time. It was the process of allowing movement to emerge spontaneously out of that deep-water well of impulse that lies beneath the level of the thinking brain – a surrender that gives into a state of profound coherence, a kind of grace, in which one thing flows into another, and meaning does not filter down from the clever brain but presses up through the surface of the skin. When we attend to inner arising like this, we are participating in what Emilie Conrad calls a first order experience – or direct apprehension.[17] Right there is a stream of movement that unfurls and unfurls the little coloured flags – the pink, the green – endless and always surprising.

Actually, there was something else, too. As a five-year-old I already knew about unfurling the flags, but I thought I was the only one. I also thought that what I was doing could only be a private act, like masturbation. It carried the same dismal wreath of shame. The 5Rhythms™ showed me that there were whole communities of of people dancing across the threshold, and that this crossing in body was a practice with a history and a name (several of them in fact).

You capsize my boat

Here I am paddling my little coracle, absorbed in my own process of inquiry, and here comes your instruction like a great big left-side wave and turns me over, leaving me gasping for air in the sea. I have mostly felt interrupted by teachers' directions on the dance floor. Even if they're couched in invitational language, they still cause a breach. Partly, perhaps, this is because I'm Autistic. It's hard for Autistic people to suddenly shift our attention. It's as if we're driving a juggernaut and we can't simply swing it around.

I don't mind if you tell me exactly what to do: ballet, ashtanga. Clear structures are good. What I mind is when you tell me I can do what I like, so I spin away, and just when I am completely absorbed in my own investigation, you insert a direction. I cannot cope with the ambiguity of this kind of experience. Either structure and direct ... or free me up to follow my own trajectory. It reminds me of times when I tried to have a job: I was always either not doing enough, or taking too much initiative (apparently). I don't know how you cruise that middle place. I don't even know *why* you cruise that middle place. I will never be in that big white ship; I will always be paddling my little coracle.

It's hard to know where the edge is here between choice and exclusion. I don't want to be on the cruise ship, but I also know that even if I did, I'd never cut it as crew. I wouldn't divine the things you're meant to know without anyone saying it. But on the other hand, I'd ask the questions no one wanted to hear. I'd clean the floor by crawling on my knees with a cloth when you're meant to use a mop. I'd stare into the infinity of space and prefer that to making conversation.

A forbidden vocabulary

I've always been very interested in those movements that have been edited out of the approved lexicon – the ones you should never do ... the ones that make you look hyper-sexual (dirty whore!), intellectually or motor disabled ('spastic!'), childish, sissy, autistic ... I notice that even in supposedly 'free' dance, on the whole these kinds of movement are carefully avoided. Supple, fluid, rhythmic is always preferred, or the big tribal release. These qualities are considered to be embodied. But I like the excised moves.

While each Autistic person has their own unique movement signature, there is also a commonality of embodiment among Autistic people (which other Autistic people easily recognise). Autistic writer and educator Nick Walker writes:

> If mind is an embodied phenomenon, it follows that the diversity of minds must also be a diversity of embodiments ... Autism, for example, involves distinctive modes of physicality and sensorimotor experience that are intimately connected with autistic modes of cognition.[18]

One characteristic of Autistic embodiment is perpetual motion – spinning, flapping, rocking – movements so taboo that a mountain of books, articles and videos have been produced by neurotypical autism 'experts' on how to stop us doing them. In *The Mind Tree*, a book written when he was between eight and 11 years old, non-speaking Autist Tito Mukhopadhyay explains why spinning is so vitalising for him. He writes (of himself in the third person):

> He felt that his body was scattered and it was difficult to collect it together. He saw himself as a hand or as a leg and would turn around to assemble his parts to the whole.
>
> He spun round and round to be faster than the fan. He felt so that way!
>
> He got the idea of spinning from the fan as he saw that its blades that were otherwise separate joined together to a complete circle when they turned in speed.
>
> The boy went to an ecstasy as he rotated himself faster and faster.
>
> If anybody tried to stop him he felt scattered again.[19]

Movement resolves disintegrated parts into an orderly system, like planets orbiting the sun, and that coherence is profoundly regulating for the nervous system. To me, a stream of movement often feels more like a resting state than stillness does, and I've never really understood those dancers who repeatedly lapse into stasis.

Early on in the process of Autism awareness, I realised that for me dance is a form of stimming[20], but I only quite recently became aware that stim dancing is actually a thing in the Autism community. And just like me, Autistic people have always been doing that thing, without realising that anyone else was, long before it was seen and recognised. It was a constant arising that kept moving through us. Probably it has been doing that since deepest prehistory. We all invented stim dancing. Nobody owns it.[21]

Should this chapter actually be called Stim Dance? Does the

conscious dance movement really belong to us? Certainly a very significant number of Autistic people show up on conscious dance floors, a small number of us diagnosed, Autism-identified and out; some diagnosed and closeted; and a far greater number neither diagnosed nor aware of the differences and distinctions of their neurology or of their significance. This is one of the things that can make conscious dance spaces challenging. It's super-hard to be Autistic when you don't know you're Autistic. You're struggling with difficulties you cannot quantify or define, and the available ways of coping often impact negatively on both the Autistic person and others in their environment.

The excised lexicon makes me think about Judith Scott and how she wasn't allowed the crayons because she didn't do the right thing with them – the thing that everybody expected, the parodic version of art: the house with four windows, a chimney and a garden path; dogs with four legs; flowers with big yellow petals. We're not allowed to have the movements either – the odd, unreadable ones. They scare people. But I want to reclaim those moves. The moves of innocence, the ones that preceded social parameters, the ones that overspill the categories and unsettle, the ones you cannot quite place or define, the ones that aren't supposed to have a meaning but whose meaning presses through like water from a stone and comes upon you in strange ways. The movements of my people.

Look into my eyes

I'm on a 5Rhythms™ dance floor, ten years or so ago. It's near the end of the dance, and here it comes again, *that* instruction: look into your partner's eyes. Now, I would tell someone where to look if they were about to walk off the edge of a precipice, or if we were strolling and I wanted to draw their attention to a beautiful flower or an unusual kind of dog. But I don't care for directing gaze in ways that prescribe interpersonal relationship, and I would not instruct it as a teacher. I don't think it's ethical; I think it oversteps a boundary. It also locates the teacher in a narrowly neuro-normative paradigm that excludes certain groups of people who use gaze in distinctively different ways.

Temple Grandin tells us:

> A 2011 fMRI study ... found that the brains in a sample of high-functioning [sic] autistics and typically developing individuals seemed to respond to eye contact in opposite fashions. In the neurotypical brain, the right temporoparietal junction (TPJ) was active to direct gaze, while in the autistic subject, the TPJ was active to averted gaze. Researchers think that the TPJ is associated with social tasks that include judgments of others' mental states. The study found the opposite pattern in the left dorsolateral prefrontal cortex: in neurotypicals, activation to averted gaze; in autistics, activation to direct gaze. So it's not that autistics don't respond to eye contact, it's that their response is the opposite of neurotypicals'.[22]

I experience eye contact as dazzling, like someone shining a torch directly into my eyes. It feels like drilling in my eyeballs. This isn't a psychological aversion or an emotional response; it's physical pain. Even looking at a picture of an eye produces these sensations. They aren't nice. They aren't comfortable. They don't lend themselves to listening, processing or connecting. My preference is for what I think of as looking aslant, side by side but a little inclined towards the other person, so eyes can touch in and dance out.

While it isn't natural for me to look directly into anyone's eyes, like many older Autistic people, over the years I've trained myself to hold all sorts of gaze, in all sorts of different situations, in neurotypical-mimicking ways, so on a purely technical level, I can do the eye gazing exercise really well – better than many neurotypical people. And, honestly, I've found that neurotypical people tend to see what they're expecting. They're not all that difficult to dupe. My gaze is a clever forgery, but it's never been found out.

On this occasion, ten years or so ago, I notice after a minute or so of eyeball to eyeball that my partner's eyes are beginning to tear up. And I am feeling ... at first it seems like nothing ... but if I pay attention and keep watching ... there it is: I feel pinned, like one of those asphyxiated butterflies impaled on a tiny cushion. I feel incandescent with fury, hot little flames of it, because once again I have been compromised, manoeuvred, forced (this is how it seems to me ten years ago), and the only way I know to break through this fakery and blast my way into truth is to get up and walk away ... but this is such a fundamental transgression of the neurotypical rules of intimate engagement that I do not dare.

You might think that would be one hell of a dance, and so it would, but if you have ever been in a minority, if you have ever felt the weight and surprising omnipresence – look, it's even here inside me! – of the arm that polices, you may understand why in this moment, ten years ago, I cannot stand up and do that dance. So I am left with this nasty-tasting insinuation, this snaky voice in my head, whispering that I am all wrong and that you, neurotypical person, are all right, because you have the tear of the majority in your eye, and the way my system works, this is not intimate.

Nowadays, of course, I wouldn't do it like that. Now I have a name and an explanation for the differences between you and me. Now I'd simply excuse myself or re-negotiate the parameters of the exercise: how we sit and where we look. *So easy is it then.* Unfortunately not. Stepping out invites projection: everybody's got their story. Negotiation is often met with bafflement. Either way, I may end up having to explain that I'm Autistic ... blah, blah, blah ... even if just then I don't particularly want to disclose. I mean, allistic people don't have to out themselves in order to state a simple preference. So, yes, it's still all freighted with splains and awkwardness, but at least I don't have to look into their eyes.

In any form of moving meditation practice, we hold the intention of staying with our experience, of continuing to move with and into it, of continuing to witness it, so that gradually, moment by moment, day by day, year by year, we expand our potential to include. Our bowl becomes ever more capacious. At the same time, balancing this willingness to be present to whatever arises, is a discriminating awareness that holds the potential to move us away from situations of harm and towards places, people and practices that hold out the possibility of knitting us into wholeness. When I look into somebody's eyes and experience the opposite of presence, I know this won't change if I work on it. And I know that, in any case, I don't want to work on it; I'm really happy with things the way they are. I'd like allistic teachers to do some work though. I'd like you to widen your perspective. It would be so easy for you to do this differently.

Autspace

One of the reasons I gravitate to dance floors is the opportunity to engage with people outside of neurotypical social conventions. They offer an 'other' space, in which I can read and negotiate with fluency, a space that drops suddenly and sheerly, deep into the hinterland, the silent wilderness of body knowing, where thinking mind is content to trail slowly behind. This is my natural habitat. It's the place where the real me lurks, half-concealed in shadow behind the social forms.

I've heard people say that they feel uncomfortable with the invitation into this particular kind of intimacy with partners they may know scarcely or not at all, but I prefer it like that. It feels like a cleaner and clearer form of engagement to me. In any case, a social connection does not necessarily translate into a dance floor one. Dancing has its own criteria, its own way of sorting and hooking and throwing you in. It's unpredictable and inexplicable. What it feels most like is sexual chemistry, but it doesn't correlate with that either.

There's nothing else like it when it comes: the wild joy, the furious presence that gathers and gathers, movements showering off like sparks from a Catherine Wheel. It feels like a force of nature – the way that clouds gather and continents slowly drift. If you are a creator, you cannot do this dance. This is a dance for witnesses, the patient and curious, the ones who know how to make themselves scarce while the movement pours and trickles and rumbles through.

Afterwards, when there's talking and eating, I want to lie under the table drifting in and out. Above, it's too loud to tease out a thread – music and clatter and everyone speaking at once. Above the table, is the buzzing in my head, like a headache but not a headache, that only hours later abates. I don't want to rattle back into community. I want to feel the slow ebb of the energy, to allow it to stream into something different – as if I cannot yet breathe on land, or the colours are blinding in the air; I want to coast alone in the small waves and let them wash me slowly home, to the house and the cups and saucers.

3

Ashtanga Vinyasa | repeat and return

'Why did you start yoga?' I get asked this question a lot, and I always feel as if I should have a clear-cut reply, one that makes podcast hosts smile and doesn't need footnotes: something about inspiration or peace or the correct lens dropping in the optometry machine and the whole world sharpening into focus. I don't have that kind of answer, though. It's weird, you know? It's hypermobile. It's Autistic. It's complicated. I don't really know.

To be honest, I've never been all that fond of yoga as a broad category consisting of static, isometric forms – although that's what I practised initially, because it's what existed back in the eighties. It was ashtanga vinyasa that hooked me and hauled me straight in, and where I felt like a member of the tribe. It reminded me of ballet in its rhythms, the *bandha*,[23] and the way it demanded everything.

Teachers will often tell you that yoga is about much more than *asana* (or postures). It's true that the scope of yoga as a science, philosophy and technology is vast, but for me personally nothing is larger, deeper or more pertinent than the physical practice – what I encounter when I step onto my mat: the somatic transmutation of sensations, thoughts, emotions and memories through moving and witnessing. This is what matters: repeat and return, the shuttle of the loom, jumping out, jumping back in, weaving up the fabric of my body. This repetition is a practicum. It's a body of artistic work. It is itself full and complete and all that I require.

Cut-out dolls

Although I could not have conceptualised it until much later, as a child and young adult I was desperate for embodiment. You'd think being born in a body … would mean you're embodied, right? But it doesn't. Embodiment to me has a quality of conscious in-dwelling and living through, of reflecting from the deeper reaches – some kind of Mariana Trench of mind. In pragmatic terms, it also devolves out of proprioceptive experiences – of sensing where we are in space, where our body parts are in relation to each other, where our individual body begins and ends. For hypermobile people like me, proprioception is impaired, and we are likely to have difficulty with all of the above.

When I was a child, I loved cut-out dolls. I loved that they could be collected and arranged in taxonomic order. I loved their apparent frozenness in time and space. They didn't move their arms, and the wind didn't ruffle their hair. They were stable and predictable, and that felt safe. I loved the aesthetics of colour and line, and it was important to me that these were aesthetics arranged around a body. And I loved the thick black line that contained each body, so that they were not always dissolving out, fragmenting and losing their parts in the way that I was. I wanted a thick black line like that. I wanted to feel gathered in and clearly delineated. I wanted to feel like a stable entity, not constantly scattering, but distinct and coherent.

I've written about my cut-out obsession before. It's a foundation story for me of dyspraxia and disembodiment, and it also bears on my long-time anorexia, which was in large part an attempt to manufacture a sense of consistent bodily containment of the kind that apparently auto-generated for others, but not for me. It was only much later, when I came to know more about genetic hypermobility and its relationship with proprioception, that I began to understand that my ongoing sense of dis-integration, was neither psychological nor an existential dilemma, but a physiological product of differences in the proprioceptive organs (located in the tendinous parts of muscles, in ligaments and fascia) resulting from connective tissue differences – or Ehlers-Danlos syndrome.

Just as only free, emergent movement could teach me to spin out across time, I needed an encounter with movement as form to discover my body boundaries. I craved structure and repetition: the discipline of movement. I guess this is why the selkie comes out of the sea and makes that crazy deal with the roof and the walls. Because there must be a bowl that holds the water, otherwise it runs off and evaporates, and that was what was happening to me.

I have a vague memory of creating a movement practice when I was in my early teens – and practising it. I can't remember much about what it consisted of, except that it was informed by ballet, which I watched obsessively but had never, at that point, done myself: it seemed to exist in a foreign land for which I would never be issued a visa. I think there was something that looked like a turned-in arabesque. I was dissatisfied, though.

My practice didn't have a name or an official stamp. It didn't really exist, in the same way that I didn't exist either.

Iyengar

But to answer your question in another way, the one about why I started yoga ... I went to university. There was an Iyengar yoga class in the Students Union every week. It was popular and sometimes crowded. There were nubbly turquoise mats (the only kind that existed in 1981) and a student who breezed in and collapsed like overcooked spaghetti into every posture. I remember the efforts of the teacher to introduce some sinew and texture, but she remained defiantly soggy.

Like most hypermobile people with no training in structured movement, I was *not* good at yoga. True, I could arrange my limbs in a wide variety of patterns (many of which seemed to me like comfortable resting positions rather than 'yoga'), but I struggled with left and right and lacked the stability to support and maintain upright shapes. I was utterly clueless in ways that I make an effort to remember when I encounter similar hypermobile students in my current-day teaching life. And yet I continued to go to the yoga class throughout my three years at university. It resonated with me in some dim, deep way.

Holy ground

My relationship with ballet has unrolled in rough eighteens. I started ballet at 18 or so, danced it for about 18 years, stopped for another 18, and then resumed. Strange.

As an artistic Autistic child, I loved stories, pictures and music. My mother left school at fourteen, but (like her mother) she was a reader, and we had lots of books. My parents were sort of agnostic, and I went to a primary school headed up by a fervent socialist who ousted Christianity from assemblies in favour of classical music. As a child, I thought that god was like Santa Claus, a made-up story that you had to pretend you believed in. For me, the mystical places welled up from inside. I lived in a brightness and intensity of experience that was sometimes painful.

It was this headteacher, Mr Clements, who took the third year (I think ... so I would have been nine) on a trip to Southampton Gaumont to see the then Sadlers Wells Ballet dance *Sleeping Beauty*. Of course I was entranced. What impressed me most vividly were the *bourrées* on *pointe* and the scrims that made and dissolved the forest of thorns. I also remember being told off good-naturedly by Mr Clements, sitting in the row behind, for eating sweets noisily. I remember that because I was an invisible child and was almost never told off.

It just didn't occur to me that ballet was something I could do myself. It seemed to exist in a different world, an inaccessible 'beyond', and so did the dancers. I longed for riding lessons but never ballet classes. I felt in advance (not without reason) that I wouldn't be able to pick up the steps and would be humiliated. Co-ordination, spatial orientation and managing the wet spaghetti of my body came only slowly to me.

* * *

So it was not until 1982, on the wave of the dance boom, that I joined a ballet class at a small studio which had just opened in my university town. I was lonely, confused by student social life, repelled by the loud, beer-sodden events I was meant to be enjoying, and the studio felt like a refuge. I was, as predicted, not very good at ballet, but I looked the part and I persevered.

I graduated and moved to London. It was dirty, gritty, arty and left-field, a world of squats and bedsits, post-punk fashions, phone boxes, Cranks, poll tax riots and the old Urdang Academy in Skelton St, with its concrete steps up, double doors and blue paint inside, the showers always boarded up, and the bunheads smoking outside the studio waiting for class to begin.

I mostly stood at the wall barre on the right-hand side as you walked in, next to the windows with the deep recesses, where we put our bags. The rosin box was front right, next to the piano. And I remember the people, as if I could walk in right now and they would all still be there – though the building has now been agglomerated into an up-market shopping mall, and some of those dancers were older then than I am now and are probably dead. Among the *bona fide* professionals and would-be pro's, there was Bernie, the 50-something builder, who danced as if he was wearing skis; Gerda, who seemed permanently dazed by her flight from post-World-War-II Germany; Arthur, the funny, gregarious gay guy weighed down by a vicious black dog. 'Someone should write a sitcom about this,' my friend Rebecca used to say. They should have. It was a crazy place where quite a lot of Autistic people found sanctuary.

Ballet gave me a vessel to pour my ecstasy into – one that grounded it like a lightning rod in body. It gave me a structure, a knitting pattern of steps. It gave me an invisible cathedral that felt like home. Ballet was my religion, replete with customs and rituals, priests, cardinals and communities of worship. While I felt painfully lost in the social world, out of place everywhere and adrift without the kind of mundane purpose that seemed to motivate young neurotypicals, walking into a studio I immediately knew that here were my people. I didn't stand out (too young, too thin, too limby, too bendy) as I felt that I did in civilian life. Hanging out in (what others considered) extreme positions did not attract attention. Stretching was totally normal – everyone constantly needed to scratch that itch. I didn't have to hide or explain this part of myself. I was anorexic, Autistic, unable to go to a party, engage in a romantic relationship, or hold down a job. Ballet saved my life.

I notice that I'm reluctant to write about this phase of my life, even though it's important and it lasted a long time. A part of me is ashamed of that poorly functioning Autistic young woman who tried so hard to make herself look neurotypical. I was strange in so many ways, and all of them felt humiliating. I completed a PhD and turned it into a book. I published articles and journalism. I pieced together a living from here and there. But I had chronic eating disorders and my mental health was not good. There are many things I won't tell you about this time in my life.

* * *

Why, you are probably thinking, is ballet in the ashtanga chapter? Well, it's because to me, they are of a piece – much more so than ballet and dance movement. They share non-negotiable structures and patterns that roll out exactly like so. Both demand dedication to the exclusion of all else – or so it seemed to me back in the day – a dedication you can lose yourself in. It simplified life; so much else could just disappear. And both ballet and ashtanga are grounded in rhythm and regularity, which contained me, relieved me of the sense of being like a dry pea in a shoe box, rattling and groundless.

I left ballet in the end because I felt I'd outgrown its preoccupation with surfaces, and ashtanga seemed to offer more of the same but with an added inner purpose. I also felt that at 38 maybe I was getting too old to *plié*. (Little did I know what ashtanga had in store!) Perhaps I was also fed up with the discrepancy between me and the people who did this for a living. (Although there were lots of amateur dancers, there was no above-water adult ballet culture at that time. We felt laughable and not legit.) And so I launched myself into something different but equally physically demanding and intense.

Ashtanga grabbed me immediately, for better or worse. I loved its patterns of repeat and return ... repeat and return. This was a serious practice, not for the faint-hearted, and more like dancing, to the rhythm of my own breath, than yoga. I felt a sense of belonging here that eluded me in other yoga settings. These, too, were my people. I was bitten and smitten.

I never imagined that I would return to ballet, although I continued to *plié* and *tendu* through my dreams as if I had never left the studio, sometimes late for class and panicking to find my shoes, sometimes spinning easily into multiple turns and levitating through *grand allegro* in ways that I never got anywhere near in real life. My body remembered all the patterns and dynamics; it remembered the back left-hand corner, near the door, drawing up on the four-in on a rising tide of nervous excitement, like a race horse about to accelerate out of the starting gate, travelling in formation across the wooden floor and into infinity.

Same, same

Stepping onto my mat to practise ashtanga is a bit like getting on a train: the rattle of the tracks, the stations unfurling in fixed and familiar order. If I mix up the sequence, the postures are often often unexpectedly harder to accomplish. While the switch may make sense on a cognitive level, my body struggles to compute. I begin to feel subtly, or not so subtly, disembodied. The predictability of the series appears to enhance proprioception, or perhaps stands in for it. If I change my mat or my orientation in the room, it's similarly difficult for my body to know where I am in space – as if I've suddenly landed on a new planet with a different gravitational field and distracting blue trees.

One thing that most allistic people know about Autistic people is that we like predictability. I think that allistic people generally understand this preference as an aspect of personality or temperament. In reality, though, it's about making it easier to navigate the world with a sensory system that quickly gets overloaded. If I wear the same outfit every day, it's because it has already met the criteria for appropriateness in all the situations I'm likely to meet. The seams don't chafe, the stumps of cut-off labels don't dig in, I can sit on the floor in it, the colours are clean and don't make my teeth feel buzzy, the patterns don't writhe in a horrifying way, the lines are pleasing, I can easily add a layer or take one off ...

Autistic people are detail-oriented. That's another thing allistic people usually know about us. It's not quite how it sounds, though. For us the parts do not easily unify into the whole in the way they do for you. Experience doesn't come bundled up. Think of a pointillist painting. You stand a few feet away and you see a little red dog, water, sailing boats, bathers in the sun; move closer ... and closer ... and the image dissolves into a snow storm of coloured dots. You see the woods, we see the trees – the undulations in the bark, the twittering of the leaves.

I like ashtanga because it's always the same. Except it isn't. The sequences don't vary, but every practice experience is unique and unpredictable. Setting the template fixes things enough that I can dwell in the intricacies of this. It's like planting a square on a patch of earth so you can count the insects. Here they are, the thousands of tiny disparate things, the fast and the slow, the brown and the iridescent, the ones with wings and the dwellers in soil. So many different eyes and feelers and surfaces. So many worlds.

Whose practice is it anyway?

In the early years, I considered myself in service to the practice of ashtanga. Like some kind of vestal virgin, I took the sacrificial view. It was a long time before I began to understand that the practice is a box of tools that belongs to me. I can use my hammer to bang in a nail or knock down a wall.

On the other hand, I've always had an ambivalent feeling about spiritual teachers. When it comes to the inlands of experience, I prefer to be an explorer than to take the guided tour, to travel at my own pace and on my own trajectory. I want my questions to roll around the deeper caverns inside, and responses to filter slowly through.

Nevertheless, when I'm practising ashtanga, it often feels to me as if there's a little old man squatting just on the periphery of my vision, tutting and gesticulating. He wants to bring me into line. He wants to tell me what to do. I don't really care about the old man. A little dog knocked his screen over long ago, and we all know that it was the journey that honed courage, wisdom and love, not his special drink, or his bran-and-pins-and-needles brain, or his silk-and-sawdust heart. But there he still is waving his arms as if he thought no one realised.

I love teaching myself. I taught myself Russian when I was fifteen, and I have taught myself Sanskrit. When I can follow my own thread, mark out for myself the territory and press into the margins of my own curiosity, I feel liberated, as if there is finally enough room to extend and breathe. Autistic people are often autodidacts, highly focused on our own interests, self-sufficient and happy to do things for the most part alone.

I've always wanted to pare things down. A mainspring of anorexia for me was the desire to resolve to what is essential, to uncover that core of inner meaning that lies irreducible in the bones of things. I would really like to be an anchorite. Every time I unroll my mat, I feel as if I'm rowing to the island: seabirds, rocks, unpredictable tides, and folded into the familiar wilderness, the tiny daily surprises.

Since menopause, I've felt a natural closure of my body. I've become again taut and self-sealed, private like a child, my fluids, my oceans contained inside. I feel the power in clean edges. It's a phase for sloughing things off — gesticulating old men, for instance — and composting the debris. There's a different kind of porousness here too, to seasons and birds, rain clouds, trees, bodies of water, big skies ... But there's also the kind of 'no' that lives within whitewashed walls alone. It sees you, and it doesn't take prisoners.

Entrails

This is the sea, the white foam horses rushing on and on, the battering wind, the pebbles flung, the starfish beached – too many to throw back in. Everything is roaring. I don't know if I want to be an anchorite. The clean white spaces seem too small and shell-like, infinitely torquing in upon themselves.

A few weeks old, my son slept like a small archbishop offering benediction. It's the coming in and the going out that slays me, like little lights, the dawn and the dusk. It's the short, roiling life of the ginger cat. It's everyone being in the wrong generation, my mother where my grandmothers ought to be, myself the keeper of the house, dealer in practical things, magician of the deluding smoke of perpetuity. My mother's house has vanished away.

The anchorite acts as if life were as clean as a bone. To her it's the string of the mala that matters, not the beads, the generations rolling through your fingertips. I tried to pay attention to the string. I adopted Buddhist practices, but impermanence only ever made me anxious. Scared to live and scared to die. The rock and the hard place. The human situation.

I could never sit still and watch the tides pouring in and out. They invited me to sift and roll and sigh. I think that Buddhism does not give enough space for the howling emotions, the ones that rip through you with their hungry wolf teeth. The child grows up and leaves. The mother dies. I want to be totally done over by the grief. I want to stamp and cry. I want to be flung up on a sandbank spitting starfish with bladderwrack wrapped around my fingers, and salt scouring my tongue.

Porridge

Like a day in heather with a clear sky and tussocky grass.

Like a clear run.

I wasn't expecting this when I woke up muscle-sore from yesterday's endeavours and intending only to glance over the surface. But then I surrender and the possibilities expand. I know it happens like this, but still it always comes as a surprise. When it's a trick I try to play on myself it never works — not quite like this — although playing injured, even when not, was a way I made this practice tractable again, malleable, like a good dough. And then I was in, away and laughing.

The edge is always going to be a challenge — stepping just so on the rope, the pole finely balanced, not a teeter left nor a totter right. Even now, with all that I know, I still have to have just a taste out of Daddy Bear's bowl — just the littlest bit — though it's Baby's porridge I actually eat. And I'm always the littlest bit burned.

If nothing was burning, if there was not this low tide of pain ebbing into sensation, so I don't quite know the name of it really, this hum … If not, would I know I was alive? It stands in for the missing proprioception. Comforting. Reminding me that I am in this body, that it has boundaries, that there is me and not-me, and other people can see. It reminds me that I am still coasting the surf of this wild sea. By some extraordinary grace, today I am here.

A mandala made of sand

Now that I'm older and a bit arthritic, ashtanga is a way of staying one step ahead in the march of time. It's a way I keep my boat riding high out of the water. Then the small pains, the little restrictions, aren't there much in ordinary life. I wish I'd known when I was younger what it really takes to keep the boat afloat. We didn't realise back in the day. In ballet it was the same. Dancers danced. Ashtangi's thought that lifting weights was cheating.

What I'm going for when I practise is less a posture than a feeling. It's like my great-grandmother's musical box: gears whirring, the prickly metal drum rolling and plinking the tiny keys. It's finding how to play the tune the way my body likes, the way that oils the works. Then there's a sense of ease in the effort. Then I become both the mechanism and the music, and the series unrolls like waves.

It isn't that I can no longer accomplish challenging postures – they approach and recede from day to day; it's more about holding all of it lightly. With Ehlers-Danlos, it's always been a bit like this, not forging ahead, but looping around and around. I'm much stronger now, though, and I'm also much happier to be in the flow of things. There's a relief in yielding to the reality of the moment, a relaxation. Every yielding creates a space, and every space invites a possibility. There's an easing of surface that allows the underlying texture to press through – roots, beetles, mulch, stones – something subtler, richer, more varied and surprising. I could fight for old territories, but I don't want a war in my body. Sometimes a posture floats back into my ambit – and another one floats away. It's funny, it's unpredictable. It's all so bloody liberating!

There's a view out there in the ashtanga group-mind that this practice is about transcending our limitations. For me, it's always been about meeting mine. There's a softening that goes with acknowledging the inherent limits involved in being human. Expansion comes when I'm able to recognise that less may be more here, and it's most helpful to pause, rest, backtrack, let go into the cyclic nature of things.

We're all in process, and sometimes ashtanga is only a staging post in a life's trajectory. You can move on or you can stay, and you can take what you learned and apply it elsewhere. This is good and healthy and alive. Me and ashtanga, we're in it for the long-haul, as far as I can tell. Gymnastic ability, on the other hand, is a time-limited commodity. It will definitely diminish and eventually cease. If the capacity to perform physically demanding sequences of *asana* is what we think ashtanga is, we're all looking forward to exile from the warm circle of the tribal fire.

I want to be in Mysore rooms that are not only leavened by the energy of the young, but also grounded and stabilised by the presence of elders, rooms where practice is flexible and adaptable, because then it can be sustainable for everybody, all the time. Increasing capacity is only one half of a practice life. You haven't finished when you've summited the mountain. Descent, dissolution and ultimately death: this too is a phase in practice – perhaps the most important one of all. Me, I want to go laughing and stumbling down the shadowy side, rolling like a drunken monk wrong-footed on the scree.

4

Hypermobility | tissue paper and glass

I started moving as a practice because I really wanted to be embodied – to feel that I was *in* my body. I couldn't have articulated it that way at the time, though. It was more of a dim uneasy sense, scratchy and confused. When I was young, a lot of energy went into holding this entity, myself, together, into being the sum of all its parts. That was why good hair and shoes were important. They held the line: the bottom and the top. Perhaps this sounds strange to people with typically coded connective tissue, but if you're one of the merry band of zebras, people with a genetic connective tissue difference – a hypermobility syndrome – you'll probably get it at once.[24]

It worked. These days I am effortlessly 'here'. I no longer dissolve around the edges unless I want to. I no longer have to look in a mirror to check I'm not invisible. I'm still not quite like you, though. My collagen will always be off; I will always have to do the work to keep my borders in place.

This chapter is about about the long, slow process of creating – and then maintaining – cohesion in a hypermobile body. It's about whispering the wild horses. It's about the agony and the ecstasy ... and learning to live in the quiet place in between. In Tibetan Buddhism there is a class of teachings called *terma* – encoded texts that lie hidden within natural objects. I feel as if my body is a *terma* – a teaching text written in muscles and bones and chromosomes. Every day I get out of bed and put myself in motion in order to unspool a little more of the meaning.

> *So nam di yi tam chay zik pa nyi.*
> By the merit of this practice may all receive wisdom.

Crazy wisdom body

For a period of my ashtanga life, I referred to my practice as 'the path of pain'. I was joking, but not entirely. The path of pain had nothing to do with masochism. I tried very hard not to hurt myself and I got intensely frustrated when I hurt myself anyway. The more I endeavoured to move 'forwards', the more I seemed to be pressed 'backwards' into a situation increasingly 'limited' by injury.

I was told that ashtanga injuries are the result of aggressive practice, and so I believed that in some subtle way, beneath my conscious awareness, I must be forcing my body. But this was puzzling because I would watch more robust types pushing themselves obviously much harder than I did or could with no apparent deleterious effects. I felt guilty and wrong, but I didn't know how to be right.

I don't remember exactly when it began to dawn on me that I was hypermobile. I was formally diagnosed with what was then called 'Ehlers-Danlos syndrome (hypermobility type)' in 2007, by Professor Rodney Grahame.[25] By then, it was confirmation of what I already knew. When Rodney asked me what I wanted to get out of diagnosis, I said that I would like to be able to set better boundaries for myself. What I meant was that I wanted to believe myself; I wanted to give weight to my own experience; I wanted to move into my own internal authority and be able to proceed consistently from it.

I have osteoarthritis, tendonitis, triggered trigger points, over-stretched ligaments, frequent minor subluxations, and only half a right medial meniscus. On paper it looks like a lot of stuff; you might think I'd be tootling around in a mobility scooter, and if I'd problematised my 'symptoms' perhaps I would be. But in actuality I walk and dance and swim and practise ashtanga. I'm fit and strong, and pain doesn't feel like pain in the troublesome sense. I could choose to relate to my body as a series of pathologies, but I prefer to understand it as a ground of fluidly arising phenomena – and to get interested in these in an open way. I've found that curiosity is a doorway to a spacious kind of peace. Does this mean I'm not disabled by hypermobility? It depends what you think 'disabled' means. I have to do a shedload of mental and physical work to maintain reasonable physical capacity, and even then my capacity can never really equate to that of someone with genetically standard connective tissue. If disability denotes the investment of time and energy in all of that, and the impact of that investment on my ability to socialise and earn a living, then, yes, I'm disabled. If it means I'm a miserable, helpless victim of my errant physiology, no, definitely not.

Buddhist mythology tells us that throughout his life the Buddha received regular visits from the demon-god Mara, bearing doubt, discouragement and temptation of every kind. Each time Mara arrived, the Buddha's servant, Ananda, wanted to bar him entry. He was, in Ananda's eyes, the daddy of all bad influences. But every time, the Buddha welcomed Mara in, greeting him with the words, 'I see you, Mara' and inviting him to sit down for tea. Pain became a path for me when I started inviting my body for tea – not the fictional body, but the one that actually exists, with its tender joints, strung-out hamstrings, travelling carpals and all the rest. Because the reality is that none of these things is a distraction from my practice or an obstacle to it; they are themselves the stuff of my practice, the royal road to enduring presence out of which flowers a particular kind of resilient joy.

In contemporary Western culture, the 'yoga body' – lithe, toned, gymnastically flexible and strong – is much desired, as if this body were in itself a sublimation, a way out of the human condition with its promise of ageing and death. That the yoga body is also imaginary and therefore ultimately never attainable makes it the ideal commercial product. The sexed up, slimmed down fantasy bodies of advertorial are constantly shoved in our faces, while we much more rarely encounter images of actual bodies doing actual yoga – or text describing the process of yoga as a real experience. Those of us who teach yoga are both products and promulgators of the industrial yoga machine. We, too, may sell the practice of yoga as a route to bliss, love, radiant health and a younger-looking body. We seldom offer an honest perspective on the complexities involved in the relationship between the process and results of practice, or of the intersections of yoga practice with our habitual human patterns of addiction, overwhelm, neurosis, anger and pain. But this is where the juice is. This is the site of real understanding, of gathering wisdom and the slow dawn of serenity.

We are habituated consistently to prefer the fugitive promise of the dreamed-of body to the always-ready-and-waiting satisfactuality of the real one (to borrow a term from Dr Doolittle). But it doesn't have to be like this. It's a radical act to acknowledge what we're really experiencing in our bodies, on our mats, here and now. It's revolutionary and it's evolutionary. Hell, yeah! Let's do it, people! Let's put the kettle on, crack open the chocolate digestives and drink tea with the bodies we actually have.

That injury is a teacher is almost a truism, but it took me a while to understand how profound these teachings can be. They are not simply biomechanical in nature but have also to do with how we are in our whole life, as it manifests in our body. From a certain standpoint, my body often appears unpredictable, illogical and capricious. Just when I think maybe I understand what's going on, it throws in something that knocks me completely sideways. When the only possible response is to burst out laughing, you know you're in the presence of a *bona fide* crazy wisdom teacher.

My physical technique background is in ballet, so I'm well schooled in the heroic capacity for carrying on regardless. And in a way, I'm very grateful for that training. It has been a valuable precursor to its meta-quality, which contains commitment and consistency, through rough-going as well as smooth; it's a kind of indestructible self-discipline built out of habit and commitment. Rather than forcing my body, denying pain or trying to breathe through it, this meta-quality entails getting on my mat anyway and doing what is do-able today. It invites mindful exploration of sensations and the emotional responses they evoke (or *vice versa*) without seeking to fix or change anything, but simply allowing any resolution to emerge, or not. It includes what's happening in the totality of bodymind, all parts and all systems, so that as little as possible gets swept under the yoga mat. Anger, resentment, envy, fear, grief – these too: chocolate digestives.

Being fully in our real, actual body, whether it's obviously injured and in pain or not, requires of us sensitivity, honesty and patience. It invites an awake, listening receptivity to what is – whatever it is. Because this is what's happening now, and this, and only this, is the teaching. If I frame my reality so that it's only 'good' yoga if nothing in my body hurts, I'm always going to be in the wrong, partly because I'm genetically hypermobile so some degree of pain and general malfunction is tantamount to a given, no matter how or what I practise; partly because as a human being it's a dead cert I'm going to encounter the full range of human experience. We breathe in, we expand, we integrate, we grow; we breathe out, we contract, we dissolve and die. A holistic yoga practice is a process of creating a container big enough and elastic enough to include all of this – all of this.

Orthostatic

When you cannot breathe; your ribs do not expand,
Your brain is full of cotton wool,
You cannot lean into your strength or go full pelt ...
Your head is fizzy as new lemonade,
And you are spinning like a leaf caught on a spider's thread ...
When the blood is labouring like an overladen sherpa to the summit of your heart –too slowly and not enough ...
You realise that you have not sufficiently migrated from your horizontal ancestors, the fish. You miss the ancient skin of water that holds you in. You think that gills were better.[26]

Post-viral

Here it is again, the bad guest, the unwelcome friend: that swooping, sliding feeling – of being a little submerged, but occasionally also shot through with light, and the sense that somewhere there is a density of body, a texture, but I cannot grasp it and crawl in. So here I lie boneless on the seabed, out of the rhythm of my tides, the odd slow current riffling my fins.

It seems unlike the selkie's water here – murky, green, obfusc. But I feel the selkie down here, moving cloudy, slow and hidden in the waving green. It seems stagnant, but it isn't really. I know what is required: to feel this in my blood and bones and limbic brain, to let it in, surrender. Then the water will heave and the selkie will shatter through.

When I must go here – and I go wailing and protesting every time, trying to convince myself it isn't so, even though I've been here a hundred times and I know the score ... When I must go here, I'm like Inanna visiting the Underworld. Ereshkigal is here, terrible, stripping me of everything I thought I owned. She makes me think of the teetering impermanence of all of this, balanced on the finest blade – the implausibility that it should be just perfectly the way it is: fingers, roof, cat, legs, son, lavender bushes, a bunch of identities, paper and pen.

Really I know I am training to die. This is what ashtanga is for: the ramping up of capacity followed by the slow, slide, the gentle gradient. I do not want to die. I do not want to be null and atomised, flying up in feathers of birds and leaves of trees, sinking into sediments of soil. I want to hang on to this crazy concatenation of circumstances by which I came to be, exactly like this. The miracle. The wonder of it.

Captain Frodo

I once heard an interview with the contortionist Captain Frodo (a.k.a. Rubberman), whose act involves fitting himself into tiny boxes and passing through an unstrung tennis racquet. He explained that he has a diagnosis of Ehlers-Danlos syndrome and that he had learnt how to dislocate and 'relocate' his joints at will when he was a child. This seems to me a very clever neurological adaptation, because in my experience dislocating is like touching fire. I'm out of that place much faster than I can think. My body knows where its parts are meant to be, even if it's sometimes a bit rubbish at keeping them there.

Three days ago, I made an awkward movement while adjusting my left foot in *ekapada sirsasana*. There was a clunk on the right side that felt an awful lot like my SI joint subluxating. The immediate sense was a kind of suspension: a long second or two of grace before sensation surged in, and with sensation testing and assessing, seeing what I could move and working it out. I know those clunks. I know that pain and immobility arrive like a caravanserai, slowly, throughout the day, one camel at a time.

For the rest of the day I felt skinless. I could hardly bear the shiver of feeling. Sounds were acute, grazing, shocking. Inside was grey, grainy, gauzy, like the spaces through an old net curtain ... like winter trees scribbling across the sky, cross-hatched and mobile. Still, now, that membraneous feeling comes and goes. It's a bit like having bad flu: tiny sensations are enormously expanded: clean sheets like an iceberg; turning over, the revolution of a planet from night into day.

I often feel as if I'm made out of tissue paper and glass. But when I'm in the thick of practice – at the deep beating heart of it – I feel melted into a fluidity in which all my parts coalesce.

There's a sense of resolving into an entity that isn't about surfaces but coheres from the centre outwards. I really believe in moving, no matter what. The more limited I am, the more important it feels to me to get up and move what's available. As I get older, I see how well the credo of movement has served me over the years. For one thing, I've witnessed the trajectories of hypermobile people who don't do this. More significantly, areas of restriction, injury, places where continuing feels impossible … these have been the sites of the most fundamental learning for me. It's a sort of recalibration that happens *in* my body but not just *to* my body. It's a whole-person event.

I'm not talking about what used to be euphemistically called by ashtangi's 'an opening' – a kind of willful breakage, often by 'adjustment' (some might call this assault). I'm a careful practitioner and not one for pounding away. It's the subtleties that capture my attention. Nevertheless, injury is inevitable now and then: partly because I'm hypermobile; partly because I'm working – out of a secure foundation of established practice – into a territory where I don't totally know. It's risky. It's unpredictable. It's life. We're always proceeding on the basis of imperfect knowledge. This body teaches me about the inherent fragility of all of that, the essential precariousness.

When a joint subluxates or dislocates, it's sympathetic alarm cry that causes muscles to clamp and bones to get stuck in the unusual places. What an extraordinary nervous system facility Captain Frodo must have … lucked into … or evolved … that he can calm the whole thing down. I wonder if the Captain also knows how to liquify his own anxiety. It seems that his capacity to box and unbox himself could be close to the kind of unattached presence sometimes considered a spiritually awakened state. Meanwhile, I sit patiently in my little boat adrift on the sea of time, patiently waiting for the tide to turn. Eventually it will wash me gently to shore.

Magic

I remember when – a decade or two ago perhaps – it was whispered that David Swenson[27] lifted weights. The shock of it, the horror! As if he was somehow cheating at ashtanga. Thank god our understanding of biomechanics has come on a bit since then. Much of the ashtanga community would now agree that cross-training is not only beneficial to the accomplishment of *asana* but also essential in maintaining healthy movement patterns over the long term. To no section of the ashtanga-doing population is it more crucial than to those of us with genetic joint hypermobility.

Mostly now in my ashtanga practice the physical gains come from outside – from body conditioning, Pilates, light weights ... These things provide substance, ballast, a grounding in strength and stability. I've put in a ton of effort there, but when I experience the results in practice, it always seems like magic.

It's obvious really, but for a very long time I didn't make the connection between doing strength work and becoming strong. To get how such a thing could be, you have to understand what it's like to be young and dyspraxic. It isn't just that you can't tell your left foot from your right; it's also that you don't know what all the different sensations mean. You're living in a kaleidoscope of shifting pieces. It was years and years before I began to be able to decode it all a bit.

The magic thing about strength training is that it turns on proprioception, so not only do you get stronger because you're lifting your tin of beans, but you start to use muscles in more functional ways. It's as if rather than you having to try to work it all out, the muscles start telling you. I used to have all sorts of little tricks and tips and images to make this one or that switch on. I still have these, but my body has become the ringmaster. A tip of the topper, a flourish of the whip, and all of that gangling, milling and lolling resolves into the fluency of acrobats and white horses trotting.

Once I was a ramshackle pile of objects, held in precarious relationship only because each one was stacked against the other. Once I was out on a limb and dancing on the brink of the precipice. It was as if my body was happening to me, but I was nowhere to be found inside. Now there's a through line. There's a kind of rising and expansion. It feels organic. It feels secure. It makes me feel alive in a different way than before.

5

Teaching, Facilitating, Therapy | a womb, a limbeck

I've always felt very clearly that teaching, facilitating, holding space is a practice in its own right. It certainly has always been that for me. This meta-practice exists at the intersection where the private inward spaces of my own personal practice encounter the private inward spaces of yours. When these two things meet they create a third thing, and that's where the juice is. This is what we are facilitating really when we work with movement: relationship. Everything else is just a pretext for that.

When I mentor teachers, there's often a feeling that difficulties in teacher–student relationships are an obstacle to get rid of so that the teacher can move on to the real business of teaching, which is assumed to exist somewhere less perplexed and more elevated. But I feel that these challenges are themselves the stuff of a teaching life – or at least a big part of it. They're the place where we actually meet our students, the learning edges that enable us to grow. Students should not always be rapt with attention and in thrall to the knowledge of the teacher. They should be antsy, unruly and reactive sometimes.

Being a teacher means being ready for the turbulence and disorder, as well as the sublime wisdom, kindness and generous presence of the real people who are our students. It means being confident in the capacity to hold a safe space for the painful and unhelpful things to unravel and, hopefully, in the crucible of practice time, knit themselves up itself into something different. Teachers often protest, 'I'm not a therapist', but you don't have to be a therapist to hold a compassionate and coherent container with safe consistent boundaries; you just have to be a solid human being and a compassionate witness. When we stand in both the strength and the vulnerability of that, we radiate hallowed ground.

A space roped off in time

What I'm good at is creating conditions for clay to morph into form: for dances to unfurl, for process to unravel, for that shifting and reconfiguration to occur that moves towards the resolution of complex trauma. In other words, I'm a lot less engaged in teaching people things than I am in holding space for experiential practice to occur.

A practice space is magical, psycho-active, charged, transporting. It can be an alembic: where you go to condense and distill. It can be your laboratory. Or it can be like a womb, strong but elastic, a place to stretch and grow but also feel the muscular containment of the walls.

To hold this kind of space requires both an energetic assertion and a set of practical actions: ways of being, doing and saying that make the container coherent and secure. Over the years, I've acquired skills, developed stamina and grown integrity, but the fundamental capacity ... I'm pretty sure I brought it with me. It's an artistic capacity, I feel; I use it also to hold the space where a book will appear or a piece of poetry. It doesn't need to insert itself. It's willing to wait silently for the wildlife to materialise out of the trees.

Teaching as presenting, on the other hand, is really not my thing. I'm not the person to stand up front and deliver a neatly tied and folded package of information. It's not that I don't know stuff, but it's hard to speak well when you think in images. The pinball machine of language is too slow, I get panicked, lose my scripts, become inarticulate.

For me, teaching in the guise of purveying information limits the scope for relationship. It precludes the intimate and surprising journey of exploration and discovery. We live in a culture obsessed with trading 'facts'. It feels like standing in the middle of an ancient battlefield as the arrows slew back and forth. We have enough arrows in our armoury to slay all the kingdoms, but a dearth of that embodied wisdom that enables us to live in harmony with the natural environment and to nurture the ecology inside ourselves. In the yoga world, one way that this essential lostness manifests is in the plethora of courses for teaching absolutely everything. How many of us slowly feel into our experience and evolve our own practicum any more? Of course, we all have to survive in the market economy, and there's nothing inherently wrong with sharing what we know, but commodification changes things.

I'm definitely not an instructor, and I feel offended when this term is applied to what I do, although I know it's only ignorance, or thinking out of a smaller paradigm. I'm not here to give directions. I don't have a recipe for a cake, or a step-by-step assembly guide. I have an invitation into some moments roped off in time, a place to come wholly, to feel and to be, to enter into the everyday cathedral of your body.

The experience you should be having

A dancer whose conscious dance practice had been mostly with me moved away. She tried a few local classes and reported back: 'Why do the teachers micro-manage it?'

When I'm teaching dance movement, my primary role, as I see it, is to create the conditions for dances to emerge spontaneously. This means establishing a container that is both robust enough to hold safely and elastic enough to include whatever arises. Of course, I will step in where the process gets stuck, but I want to put in only the smallest sketch of a gesture, the littlest I can. I want to get out of the way as much as possible so that what happens is *your* dance, *your* experience, and I am a quiet witness.

I teach like this because as a dancer I have myself always sought out settings that offer a secure container for dances to arise on their own. They have that natural levity – that power of self-levitation. But, to tell the truth, I've more often been marshalled and chivvied and told what I should be experiencing. Perhaps this is because it's much easier to teach like this. You can feel as if you're doing something, that you are the one with the magic beans, and you are in control. To hold the kind of space in which you don't know what's going to happen, and you don't try to kindle, coax, shape or manipulate it … in which you stay present to the process that's actually happening and trust that inherent within it is the unfolding that needs to happen … This takes courage and a lot of capacity. On this dance floor, it often looks as if the teacher isn't doing much, but actually this invisibility, this quality of 'nothing' is exactly what the teacher *is* doing.

Within both the 5Rhythms™ and the Open Floor movement practice, I've repeatedly heard about the importance of TEACH-ING and BEING TAUGHT. And this is one reason why, as a space-holder and facilitator, I am not aligned with either of these organisations. For me, this kind of teaching as instructing is putting a lot of furniture in the room and insisting that people sit on it, or at it. I'm not, as a point of principle, against creating structures like this, because I know that there are people who respond well to this way of framing things, but I do object to the refusal to accept that for some of us the furniture gets in the way of having any kind of deep, authentic or meaningful experience.

I've heard – a lot – from teachers in the 5Rhythms™ and the family of dance practices descended from it, that 'just dancing' (notice that 'just' – pejorative, isn't it?) is inferior to submitting oneself to 'teaching'. In other words, immersion in process is lesser than receiving external content. Sounds bonkers, doesn't it? One senior teacher speaks about dancers who come week after week, year after year, to unfacilitated classes, where you can 'just dance', and nothing in their dance ever changes. And I think, so what? I think, perhaps they didn't show up feeling that their dance needed to change. I think, for 'change' read 'improve'. I think, in whose eyes? I think, how do we know what a dancer is experiencing and what might be shifting for them? I think, or are we projecting? I think, does the dance, and the intention of the dancing, belong to the teacher or to the dancer, and are we trespassing when we make a judgement here?

Autistic dancers are at high risk of falling into the 'needs to improve' category. In order to remain within in a healthy window of tolerance, we may prefer to dance mostly alone. We may be unable or choose not to make eye contact. We may look stimmy. All of these things are highly open to misinterpretation by neurotypical teachers, and as a result, we are often seen as 'resistant' to the general project.

For me, describing a dancer as resistant is really a way of shutting them down. It's a way of not owning that there's a project in the room – an invisible set of rules and goals and expectations. Because if there weren't, what would there be for the dancer to resist? You can pretty much guarantee that the 'resistant' dancer is bringing in those things that the school or the teacher or the practice container has not, so far, been broad enough to encompass. If the container is any good – if it's vital, generative and evolving – it will respond to challenge by growing. If it isn't, well, blow that for a game of soldiers.

A bunch of wild flowers

Yoga is not the architecture of postures. It's what happens in the encounter with them. This process of meeting is designed to bring to light our conditioned responses (known in Sanskrit as *samskharas*), and it's here that we are invited to offer our attention. A yoga mat is a very revealing place to be. How we show up there is how we show up as a whole human being – not just the parts that we know about, the ones in full light and plain sight, but the mysterious dark and floating ones that lie below the water line.

As beginning ashtanga practitioners, most of us are very interested in who's doing what, and whether we can do it as well as or better than they can. We may rate ourselves on our ability to jump, bend and perform technical tricks, as if we were in some kind of yoga Olympics. At the same time, in many yoga circles, the obverse view is *de rigueur*: practitioners with the capacity for very physically challenging postures are slated for their prowess, as if being able to balance on one hand makes them in some way not 'serious'. Actually, neither being 'good' at *asana* nor being 'bad' at *asana* is an index of spiritual attainment. It just isn't about that.

From the teacher's point of view, in the Mysore room I don't see ranks and levels, I see nature arising. Each person who steps into the *shala* brings with them a unique ashtanga vinyasa, one specifically adapted to their own body, life experience, age, temperament and so on. These multifarious ashtangas do not exist on an ascending scale, they exist within a broad field of arising. In a Mysore *shala*, as in any environment, we need our biodiversity in order to cultivate a balanced ecosystem.

I think that ashtanga can be much more interesting than the dogmas of a fallen guru, the wizard revealed behind the screen. It can be about Dorothy and Toto, the Tin Man, Glinda, the Cowardly Lion, the Munchkins and the Monkeys with wings. It can be the story of each of us, different and individual but gathered, like an armful of wild flowers. Then it feels various and inviting. Then it feels like something I want to be a part of.

Leaving silently

I once took part in a restorative yoga teacher training led by a well-known teacher. I knew it was going to be a big event, but you could have knocked me down with a feather when I stepped into the rather lovely high-ceilinged space and saw 200 mats.[28] This was training on an industrial scale. The hosting studio had supplied all new equipment, so the air was thick with cotton dust and off-gassing from several hundred yoga blocks. The teacher was miked, and most of the face-to-face teaching was done by assistants.

The way this training basically proceeded was: 1) the teacher demonstrated a posture with propping, and 2) we reproduced the posture and the propping in pairs (one propper and one proppee), while assistants roamed the room pointing out instances where our reproduction had missed the mark. I hated the propping. I felt trussed up like an oven-ready turkey. There was no way to move without upsetting the complex structure of bolsters, blankets, bricks, blocks and eye-bags balanced beneath and on top of my body – no way to shift and roll and breathe. I have rarely felt less relaxed.

This is an example of prescriptive rather than collaborative facilitation, and it is profoundly non-inclusive. It's a model in which students are 'done to', in which they are required to submit their internal experience to the authority of the teacher. It doesn't ask, 'What might make you feel comfortable?; it tells you that you will like it. What I wanted to do was heave off the mountain of soft furnishings and wriggle. I wanted to feel into the kind of support my body might appreciate. It seems like such a reasonable desire, such an innocent disruption. But it also shakes the foundations of a marvellous edifice and, make no mistake, there's a price to pay for that.

In hindsight, I recognise that I became situationally mute in that restorative training: I lost the capacity to communicate in meaningful ways. No one noticed, and I never went back after the first day. As far as I'm aware, no one noticed that either. Certainly no one contacted me to find out if I was OK. I wasn't.

Autistic people are trained to like it when we don't. We're told explicitly and implicitly that things always have to be the way that's pleasing for the neurotypical majority. Last night, I watched an Aucademy video about coming out.[29] All three participants recounted losing neurotypical friends when they disclosed their Autistic identity. Not because the neurotypical friends wanted nothing to do with Autistic people on principle, but because they couldn't understand why the Autistic person was no longer willing to shop in a mall, go to a dinner party, or spend an evening in the pub. They felt that if the person had previously been able to mask through sensorily disturbing and socially overwhelming events, they should be able to go on doing it. They had no appreciation of the physical, emotional and mental health costs of 'passing' in neurotypical environments. They could not 'get' that an Autistic person who has embraced their Autistic identity is no longer willing or able to pretend.

I didn't lose friends when I came out, but I did lose practice communities. I couldn't fake it in these spaces any more, and there was no way for me to participate with integrity. I knew now what it felt like to have a well regulated nervous system, and I knew that most of what went on in those communities didn't make me feel regulated. Not necessarily because it was all bad (although some of it was), but because the vast majority of it was top-down. It was more interested in imposing preconceived structures than finding out about the needs of the actual people in the room and proceeding on that basis. The job of the participant was to get on with the structure or lump it. Sometimes I got a sympathetic high from the adrenalin produced by dealing with the overload and mistook that for a kind of ecstasy that was good, but really I was profoundly disembodied a lot of the time – even when I was being seen and described as an example of someone 'in their body'. Since I came out, some communities have paid lip service to accommodation, but none of them has really changed its tune. It took a long time and a lot of heartache to come to terms with all of this, and in some ways, I haven't really yet. I'm still hoping there's a community I can feel nurtured within, where my Autistic self can fully express and belong.

I didn't just hate being trussed up at that restorative teacher training; as a teacher I felt offended at being presented with an instruction sheet and told to follow it. I felt that my capacities and my personhood were being denied. I felt cheated of that process of co-creation that happens with our students when we work horizontally. That isn't to say that as teachers we don't have skills, knowledge and experience that can be of value to our students. Of course we do. But we have to be mindful not to impose these things on them. We have to be willing to listen more than we speak, and to respond more than we initiate. We have to make sure we are not talking down from the apex of a triangle, but are in reciprocal flow with our students, receiving … offering … receiving … offering … receiving. We have to be humble, not assuming that we know better than them what they need – when actually we know next to nothing about their life experience and inner soul.

I wish I could end this piece of writing by telling you how I've become able to speak in a way that makes my needs known and creates a space for me. But in situations like the restorative training I still feel just as flattened as ever. I mean, where do you even start? I've solved the problem by not engaging with workshops and events – excluding myself before somebody else excludes me. If I were in the restorative training situation today, I think I'd still leave silently.

No, I'm not comfortable with that

I've never been officially assessed for pathological demand avoidance (PDA), but I'm aware that I'm an Autistic person with a PDA profile. 'You always say no', a friend's husband once told me, and he was right: 'no' was how I navigated the world, a default position. But I also conceded way too much through masking, 'passing' and giving in to the crushing inevitability of the Daleks. I didn't think I had a choice. 'No' was not a legitimate right to self-determination; it was the secret defiance of the population of an occupied land, the resistance of the oppressed.

Autism advocates have redefined PDA as a 'pervasive drive for autonomy'. That makes sense to me if 'autonomy' translates as a right to determine my own boundaries, to maintain the thin black line around my edges – to exist. I would redefine PDA as a 'profound desire for authenticity'. For me, 'no' was a back-handed, under-side way of constructing a self and protecting it against all the pulling and pushing of the world, its endless manipulations, a snail shell, fragile and paper-thin.

I recently heard an Autistic advocate explain that she'd told her daughter, 'It isn't naughty or rude to tell a teacher, "No, I'm not comfortable with that." '[30] I could have wept. What would school have been like if I'd been able to state a boundary simply and clearly like that? This kind of 'no' is very different from the reflexive one that my friend's husband called out. It proceeds out of feeling deeply into what you need and knowing that nothing is more important than that: that nothing good for anyone can come from moving forward without thorough-going consent.

In yoga and dance environments where consent is not a priority, where insufficient attention is paid to offering open choice, and processes are subtly coercive, PDA people are often seen as arsey, anarchic, resistant and unwilling to co-operate. But I think we're the canary in the room. I think we're primed to react *tout de suite* to top-down demands, overbearing approaches, tacit assumptions. I think that, if facilitators are paying attention, we can be the safeguarders of collaborative, inclusive practice.

In my view, the primary task of teachers and facilitators is to seek ways of helping students to feel into their own authenticity, and out of that authenticity to emerge self-authority. If a student is 'resistant' this should be a signal for us not that the student is behaving badly but that something is wrong with our facilitation. The space has ceased to be fluid enough; it has clotted and congealed; we are imposing information and structures rather than enabling co-creation. Possibility has closed down. This is no longer an environment that is safe for students to be real and vulnerable in, where it is appropriate to say yes.

Opening the cupboard

Have you ever had a cupboard where for years – generations even – everyone has thrown the junk they don't know what to do with? The kind of cupboard where the remnants come to rest, where obsolescence is stratified by age and weight, sifting into a mossy ground of fluff. The kind of cupboard that is the repository of every sort of broken thing, the out-of-date, dried up, decayed and useful once upon a time? When I work with a new complex trauma client, I often feel as if we're opening the door on a cupboard like this. It's overwhelming. Boxes of broken children's toys tumble off towers of tins of paint. Stacks of newspapers shift and exhale drifts of dust. Spiders run for cover. It's hard to see what's what and how one thing relates to another.

Sometimes, just knowing that you have that cupboard is a place to begin, without even needing to look inside. Maybe there's a sense of the size, shape and location, and a realisation that the cupboard has a door. We start by attending to all the ways that opening the cupboard will surely bring the house down. Chinking open the door and peeping in may happen only much, much further down the line.

A cupboard like this can feel like more than a person can bear. You may feel a violent desire to set it alight or knock it down, but axe blades blunt, tinder goes damp, and when you bring in a bulldozer, the cupboard resurrects itself. So instead we slowly, carefully, respectfully examine every little thing inside. We try to understand its history and purpose, and what its function may be now. We can start anywhere, with the first thing we see. And gradually there's a neat pile here, and another there. This can be given, and that recycled, and this can be thrown away. There's a degree of clarity, more room to manoeuvre, and the cupboard seems a bit more manageable than before.

Into the forest

It's funny how just when I'm at the point where everyone wants a piece of me, I'm already letting go, already slipping back into the forest.

I worked so hard to establish a ground of practice, showed up every day, and incrementally, without me noticing, all of it became a deep foundation. Became a body of skills and knowledge. Became integrity – you have to learn that experientially I think.

It's more than a good intention; it's a set of operational skills.

I made sure it was always all about me. That's a pre-requisite. You have to immerse yourself in your own exploration. You can't do it to become something for someone else, or all you have is an empty casket. It's said that yoga teachers are often helpers and nurturers, the ones who give too much and find themselves erased. I'm not like that. I've always experienced myself more as an artist: creator of shapes and forms, transformations, liminal spaces. As such, I'm typically pretty selfish.

I don't know what I expected from arrival, but having got here, it isn't like that. People have a strange idea of who I am, and what they think I can do for them is off. I always wanted to be truly witnessed, but instead I feel as if I've stepped into a Hall of Mirrors: fat ones, thin ones, ones with a giant head and tiny feet. None of them is a true reflection. But I find that I don't care much any more.

In the traditional yogic view, the forest is a place of renunciation, the fourth *ashrama*, the final stage in a human life, but I feel as if I already know it well, this green cathedral made of shadows and light. I feel as if it's where it all began, the branches over-arching, oak leaves mulching, decomposition, decay, new life erupting underfoot. It feels like a generative place, a place to hunker down, to pause, to drop inside, to shrug off bad reflections. I think I'll stay here for a while. I think I'll let a few things slide. I think I'll leave you grasping for that husk I've left behind, and I'll be gone, away with the tawny owl, the foxes and the bats.

6

Writing | starburst and ocean

The most important thing is writing myself down
Like a diver on the end of this rope
Into the ocean of images
That startle only slowly into starbursts of words,
Bright and sporadic, like sudden shoals of fish
Blurting into the silent world.[31]

Why is writing an embodied practice? There's a whole field of academic research engaged in exploring this question, but essentially for me it's because bodies do writing. Fingers hold pens, dance over keys, articulate with hands, arms, shoulders, into the sinews of backs. Words themselves, when excavated, dissolve into embodied experience: *excavate* (Latin): 'to hollow out or form a hole in' ... *dissolve*: *dis* + *solvere* (Latin): 'to loosen'. The stuff of writing, our experience in the world, is essentially one of being a body. It's all we know. Even our thoughts, whizzing from synapse to synapse ... even that Mount Olympus of mind ... all arises not from ether, but from tissues, offal. We can't write anything that doesn't originate in embodied experience: the seen, heard, tasted, touched.

The first piece in this chapter, 'Bleeding Words', started life in 2014. A lot has changed since then. Writing became a more easeful process for me when I realised that it wasn't any different from dancing. I could just throw out a line and follow it. It was already there to tap into rather than something I had to create. These days, I live in the quiet sanctuary spaces of post-menopause, full of birds and trees, and I don't experience writing as an erotic act. I also understand that there is a relationship between writing and the passage of time. It can't be finished before it's started. There has to be room in construction for the process of gravity, for the settling of substances and the emergence of different relationships between spaces. I like this piece though, so I have included it with only a few little changes.

Bleeding words

Ernest Hemingway apparently once said:

> There is nothing to writing. All you do is sit down at a typewriter and bleed.[32]

I may possibly not have the same relationship with bleeding as Ernest. While I think he's probably intending razor blades or knives – the clean cut, the sudden thrust – I'm getting tides, the moon and the leg-collapsing sensation of drawing down. No act here, no drama. Even the blood is not just blood but a pulp of tissues. Still, it's true there's nothing to this kind of bleeding.

And I really wish I could write that way. I really wish there were a running tap or a tide, because nothing to me is more trammelled, stilted and stuttering than making the little ants march across the big white spaces. For me, writing is more like wading through waist-high sludge than opening a vein. Many times in my life, I've said: no more. I have neither will nor stamina to unravel the mad spaghetti of my mind. And yet here I am again ... and again ...

Lord Byron explained, 'If I don't write to empty my mind, I go mad.'[33] I feel that. I often empty my mind by moving (Byron did too – remember the Hellespont?), but it's a different kind of emptying. Byron is right: there's something cathartic in tipping out the trash can. At least then you can see what's mouldering and mulching; it's no longer silently doing its inexorable organic thing inside your head. There's a satisfying sense of compensatory aesthetic control when the inchoate is mustered and corralled, penned into neat black lines and grammatical structures – even if all they really do is frame its essential wildness.

But for me it's not enough just to quietly lasso a few horses. I have this need to be heard, seen and truly apprehended, to know that I am not sifting away like sand through an egg-timer. It's as if some maniacal little Führer in my head is constantly yelling, 'Listen, all of you! Listen! Just LISTEN!' Because otherwise I don't exist. I'm whirling and whirling away, down the plughole, over the event horizon.

So, start where you are and all that, I thought I'd excavate it a bit, this feeling: the wool in my mouth, the thick tongue, gagging, choking. Just why is it so difficult? Just why?

The thing is, when I write, I do feel as if my life depends upon it, and it depends upon it being good – so I have high standards. It has to sing for me; it can't clunk or collapse with an exhausted sigh. Writing is something I do well or I don't do at all. In some ways, this urgency, this sense of life-depends-upon, begins in a response to hyperphantasia. I think in images. I *see* my thoughts, all of them, and then translate them into words. A writer friend – neurotypical – once told me she was envious of what she saw as my ability to generate images in poetry. I wanted to explain to her that I don't have to generate anything. The inside of my head is an overwhelming prolixity of multi-layered and inter-penetrating images. Images are for me the ground of consciousness. The difficulty is in sifting and sorting. It requires a huge amount of executive function, and if you're Autistic, you don't have a lot of executive function.

The first time I heard an Autistic person describe the way they think as a movie, I was puzzled. Why was this something that needed explaining? How else was there to think? I still can't conceive how it's possible to have a thought without seeing it – and then, by some special form of osmosis, receive the meaning (as you would interpret a poem or a painting). Words seem such a sophisticated product of consciousness, like an aeroplane or the iPhone, so removed from the primal mud of the source. What would it be like for thoughts to leap pristine and fully formed into language? It seems so quick and immediate.

I love films (actual ones), especially when they create their own landscape and communicate mostly through it. They are for me a form of direct apprehension: visual to visual. It's a jaw-unhingeing relaxation to inhabit this kind of instantaneous world in which meaning presses through the surface like colours in a dirty sponge and soaks unmediated into my consciousness. Sponge to sponge.

When I write, there has to be the interpolation of another surface, one that must be negotiated and surmounted, and with it comes a sense of impotence. The thing is, when you think in images, so much of everything that matters – detail, colouration, mood, tone, and a kind of slidingness between one thing and another that allows for multiplicity, for more than one thing to be true at the same time and for everything to be connected to everything else – so much of this slips though the spaces between the words, leaving you with something at best diminished, at worst tangential to its actual meaning or signifying absolutely bloody nothing.

I also feel in images. My emotional experience happens in intense, rich, brightly coloured moving pictures, saturated with metaphorical meaning. I am one of those Autistic people who experiences an overwhelming amount of emotion. There's so much going on in here that I often feel in danger of drowning in myself, and I struggle to experience a sense of containment. Like many Autistic people, I find it difficult to name and categorise emotion. Partly, this seems to be due to the sheer volume of it happening all the time. Partly, it seems to devolve from the fact that no words have been coined for many of the emotions I see-feel. They exist like outlaws beyond what is languaged, defined and accepted as a known emotional experience. I need fifty words for snow. These days, given time (I've practised a lot), I can usually match what I see roughly to a fully accredited word for a feeling, but it's a very broad category that loses much of the particularity, aesthetic wonder and intensity of the actual emotion. It communicates a lot less than it leaves out, and this is mightily frustrating.

There's another thing, too. I came here first to dance, but dancing (at least how I did it, me and Mary Hopkin) wasn't really encouraged in my family – not in the way that reading was. It felt shameful, like masturbation, an act that ought not to be seen.

So I became a secret dancer, and writing became my first public practice and discipline, the first expressive form where I was witnessed. It also became the dungeon where my dancer was tied up and hidden. While I have set her fully at liberty in the world, writing continues to be freighted for me with the frustration, limitation, dislocation / relocation of something that is not my first means but which had to be reached for, manipulated into. Maybe that's why dancing is for me much more like Hemingway bleeding: a running tap, an open vein.

Just lately I allowed myself to notice something else: writing and reading are erotic experiences. It's the name I didn't name of that intensity of being intimately read – by school English teachers and onwards to mentors and lovers I've written to. While I was fiddling around, turning the compost for this article – writer's fore-play, essential to the writing act – I typed some words I like by Matthew Remski:

> Language is continually overflowing its consensus meanings ... When we use it playfully, it co-creates with us. But when we domesticate it to a conceptual purpose, our most serious grammar and richest vocabularies become very fragile nets through which most of the world escapes.[34]

And as I typed, I was overtaken by this swoony, vertiginous feeling, of one thing collapsing into another – time, space and personhood. And for a moment I could not quite recollect ... Who do these words belong to? To me? To you? Where did they come from? And I wondered, do you press through into another person's consciousness when you re-write their words? Do you? Is it like lying naked, mind to mind, but still essentially unknowable? Are words really sex? Did my family get it all wrong?

And somehow I waded through the mud to the end – and the bit of writing I really love: polishing, refining. I'm Autistic; I'm a details person. I have no eye for the big picture, and the process of emerging a structure is laden with anxiety for me. I can't always bear to stay present for it. It's got better since I embraced the associative nature of my thinking. I no longer look for lines, but drop in a pebble and follow the rippling out. And the rippling out and the rippling out ... until the ripples dissolve into a sort of stillness.

Witness

I used to feel that nothing I wrote had ever been read enough, or correctly. I never felt apprehended. I never felt witnessed. When people read my words, I wanted them to feel what I felt and see what I saw. They never did. Eventually, I realised that the only person who will ever do that is me. It's like when I play the single same track and there are as many different dances in the room as there are dancers. I saw that in order to liberate myself I had to liberate the readers. I had to say, 'These patterns of words are yours: your hook, your prompt, your catalyst.'

I guess if you think in language, the dilemma of showing what you saw does not exist. There must be an economy in thinking like that. But how do you know the other things? The peripheral ones, and the things round the back, and the ones that are not submissible to words? These must be the people with plots and plans, the ones who go straight down the line, tacking in arguments from left and right. They do not proceed by digression because everything is connected to everything else. They are not Laurence Sterne, for whom a novel formed like a globe from a single moment and filled and filled. They are not Virginia Woolf, whom I think I almost quoted just then.[35]

I wanted to control the way people read my words for the same reason that I wanted to control my body: because I'm hypermobile and dyspraxic and it's difficult to maintain a sense of boundaried self, coalescent and not constantly disintegrating. It was terrifying to be held in people's minds as a prism of views. It felt like erasure. I'm not sure how I feel about this now. When I think about it, I still experience that sick, swooping, vertiginous feeling, the floor dropping away from beneath my feet.

Emilie Conrad says, 'What we call a body is an open-ended expression of an ongoing universal process that is in constant flux, arranging, re-arranging and experimenting, as new forms come into existence.'[36] I guess I'm a lot more OK with being a process now. There's a certain kind of relaxation in this view. It releases me from the strain of trying to contract myself into a permanent entity. This body is a single swoop down the rollercoaster: some moments sick with fear, others dizzy with ecstasy. How can you make a coherent surface out of that? All too soon, your two-bob whooping slide is up. The roustabout will lift the iron bar, and you must get up and go, although you wish it would continue forever.

Castle

In my late-teens and early-twenties, I retreated inside a castle. I have a very clear memory of writing a poem about living in it. I associate the poem with my upstairs room at 5 Hillside, so I must have been about twenty then. The castle gave a clear structure to what I experienced as my own amorphousness. It was massive and impregnable, and in hindsight I think it also protected the overwhelmed and out-of-their-depth Autistic parts of me. From the battlements I could survey the terrain without having to engage with it. I could pull up the drawbridge. These were also the anorexic parts, and the castle was a metaphor for anorexia, which I experienced as a positive thing, a life-saver. I still think it was that.

In my rosy post-menopausal late-fifties, I have come back to the castle. It's still a metaphor for my body and also now for my beloved house (the one made of mortar and London stock — I suffered so much from not having a house when I was in my twenties). But I'm living a different iteration of my relationship with the castle now. It no longer represents for me the desperate need for holding and control, but a kind of secure in-dwelling and uninterrupted contemplation. A locus to do my work. A place to spring out from and then return.

I have wondered a lot about the moat, which in the castle of my teens and twenties exiled the water outside. Now I would definitely like to swim in it. I also feel a little bored by the stillness of the water. I want it to have tides. I want it to do more than placidly mirror the sky.

I experience my house not just as a dwelling place but as an extension of my body, a second skin. It protects me from my own porousness. This morning I prised the lid off a 21-year-old tin of Rustin's Yacht Varnish (bought the first year I lived here) and varnished the wooden lintel beneath the front door, an annual autumn ritual, a spell for the threshold, weatherproofing my ship against the winter to come. And so we breast the sea.

I don't know why this piece feels to me more about writing than Autism. Perhaps because it's about the construction of something: a surface, a snail's shell. And in a way, writing is also a surface for me, a way of communicating something real and meaningful, but also making a boundary. It says: 'This that is true for me I give you freely, but do not mistake it for intimacy.' I will pull up the drawbridge and lock the door if you try to come any closer.

Archivist

My inner archivist is elderly and slow, hunched a little in his brown and green tweed suit. Keeper of the blog. Preserver of the old things. Every word a pearl to him. But really my words are so many motes dancing in a patch of light. They're not as important as all that. The archivist would like this book to be Collected Works, and in fact that would be much easier than swimming out again. (The archivist lives on land; he can't have all that paper getting wet.) This project, I tell him, draws from the old, but it's all about turning things up a different way, feeling something new.

Sometimes I wish I'd given the archivist a freer rein. For instance, I wish I still had the poem about the castle, and the diary entry in which I joined up hypermobility, Autism and ME,[37] way before anyone else was writing about the connection. All the diary entries actually. I wish I had more of my past – the inner life, not the outer – in the way I actually experienced it, not back-lit by memory. But the archivist was up against my shame and the desire to curate myself, and all of that is gone.

Hacking off the plaster

My grandfather and his brother George were known for being the best plasterers in Portsmouth. They would start at opposite ends of the room and where they met you couldn't see a join. I've inherited their talent for making smooth surfaces. Sometimes I smooth myself out out so thoroughly I'm almost obliterated.

In his article 'The Lobes of Autobiography: Poetry and Autism', Ralph Savarese, coins the term 'autie-type' for what he describes as 'a highly poetic language that many non-verbal Auties produce spontaneously on their computers, whether in conversation or in actual poems'.[38] In my experience, it's not just our non-verbal siblings for whom autie-type is a first language, but all of us Autistics who struggle with processing and producing the spoken word and find writing a lot easier.[39]

Autie-type is highly metaphorical. It's also porous. When I'm writing, I don't want to create a product so much as to allow my internal experience to press through to the surface and coalesce in words. This never happens. What emerges is a different thing and I've learnt to accept that what I want to say, what I really experienced, lives in the interstices – between the strokes, in the hollow of the O, in the curve of the C. Some examples of Autie-type:

> 1. When I was little everyone thought I was retarded. The very hurtful easy lessons I attended were time spent away from the real world. Addition, subtraction, multiplication and division were subarctic activities. Treated as autistic, retarded, and sedated, I saw myself suspended. Ashamed, I seasoned this mind of mine. Wasting time beasts inhabited my very much lost,

very sad boy's head. Attempts to freshly respond to humans were terrifying quests through killer trees. Where I sent my real self, reasonable, easy breathing, satisfying humans never could find me.

2. The wave breaks, the bone splinters, and I roll like a planet, like a perfect pearl from the conduit into the shiny vista of my life. I am afraid of the sea. At night in the one-tooth domino house she breathes my susurrating dream. I am the spray on her curling tongue, the loose knot her fingers untie. Help! I have no edges. My atoms scatter on the wave; my cells disperse like seeds. And yet I also yearn for this dissemination, the webbing of the flesh unwrapped, the rags unpinned from the bones. Torn between desire and fear, I think I will forget I am the waves, and the incoming tide is the advent of my soul. I think I will exclude this difficult sea.

3. Color – Caste – Denomination – These – are Time's Affair – Death's diviner Classifying Does not know they are – As in sleep – all Hue forgotten – Tenets – put behind – Death's large – Democratic fingers Rub away the Brand – If Circassian – He is careless – If He put away Chrysalis of Blonde – or Umber – Equal Butterfly – They emerge from His Obscuring – What Death – knows so well – Our minuter intuitions – Deem unplausible

The first passage is by Ralph Savarese's son DJ, who I think was about thirteen when he wrote it.[40] The second is by me, and comes from a prose poem called 'The Rib Cage', about my experience of being anorexic. I wrote it in my early thirties. The fourth is a poem called 'Color – Caste – Denomination' by Emily Dickinson, whom many Autistic readers believe to have been Autistic.

Reading 'Lobes' was an epiphany for me. When I first read DJ's words, I didn't know whether to laugh, cry or jump up and down. Instead, I walked around and around my house and banged the walls to let off some of the froth. The first coherent thought to bubble to the surface was: this is exactly the secret misty way words rise off images in the early morning of my mind. And the second one was: is it chutzpah or just naiveté, this materialisation of native speech on paper? Because it feels like suicide. It feels like inviting over the Daleks and saying, 'Exterminate me now!' No one reads my Autistic speaking. I make too damn sure it's all joined up and in good neurotypical syntax before it gets anywhere near a public page.

Ralph Savarese says that metaphor most usually arises from the right brain, whereas, grammar and syntax most usually arise from the left (although there is lots of variation among individual brains, with some people having functions on the 'wrong' side). A 1977 study cited in 'Lobes' suggests that 'autistic children process information predominantly by strategies of the right hemisphere from birth and, unless unusual events occur, continue to be right hemisphere processors throughout their life.' Which is why I mostly float in a mythopoeic world, tethered by a fine thread to consensus reality. I pretend to go along with the mainstream view a lot more than I really do. The Daleks again.

Word production is also lateralised to the left brain, which explains why, although superficially I appear highly articulate, in fact vocabulary retrieval is difficult for me. It's like rattling the ball through a beat-up old pinball machine, over shelves and buckled ledges, round and round the bumped-off corners, to issue somewhat randomly at other end. It's convoluted and frustrating, and it takes a lot of time. On the other hand there's creative potential in the sidewaysness of the words that tumble through. They may not be quite the ones I was looking for, but they open up a whole other train of seeing / thinking – associative and out-of-the-box.

I used to mask this difficulty – the way a stutterer covers by finding alternative words. I pivoted, reversed and went around the houses. I did it very skilfully. I don't do that so much any more. I dislike the cover-words with their lack of specificity and circumlocution. I prefer to allow the little gaps and hiatuses; I prefer to let the wrong word come: a *pet* is a *parrot*; a *parrot* is a *carrot*; *agriculture* is *agrimony* ... is *acrimony* ... is *crimson* ... This is the way I don't erase myself; I don't deface the native beauty of my own arising but simply let myself be.

It's easy to erase and deface yourself if you're Autistic, and hard to stand up and be who and what you actually are – all one hundred and extra 42 per cent of it.[41] It takes courage and a lot of practice. Autism is like the gift of a dozen wild and furious horses to hitch to your carriage. You can break them if you like – if you want them to end up mean and bridled and dispirited. It's taken me half a lifetime to whisper my horses, and it requires a lot of of skill, experience and mindful attention to keep the carriage moving forward without rattling, jostling, spooked and hell-for-leather horses, and generally pitching everyone into a rut.

I'm really committed these days to disrupting surfaces. I want to know what everything is made of. I want the materiality of lumps and bumps, coarseness and sticking out bits. I want the old bones, coins and broken tea-cups. I want what presses up out of the pores of the earth. I'm no longer so willing to small myself down and fold it up in a box because I think it might offend. I want to be full of myself.

Echoes and repeats

One of the ways I de-autistfy my writing for the page is by removing the echolalia. Echolalia is a language pattern that proceeds by repetition, through what it says on the tin: the echoing of words or sounds. You might think that that's poetry, and I would say that you are correct, but neurotypical autism experts most often describe echolalia in terms of 'dysfunction' and 'symptoms'. For them, it's a way of processing language that has to be replaced with something better.

For me, echolalia is a particular kind of thinking by association, in which the sound of one word (or a series of words) elicits the sound of another. If I've used a particular word in a sentence I'm likely to use it again in the next one, because I've felt into its pliability, into the way it can turn itself out differently in a different context or a different tense or a different part of speech. This isn't something I do consciously; it's just the way my mind revolves.

School English assumes that everyone thinks by logical deduction and that language is the vehicle for this process. Neither of those premises is true for me. Language arises for me in repeats, alliterations, resonances, rhythms and rhymes. It arises like grass and trees and birds, and just as I see grass and trees and birds, I see language. I turn it into something that can communicate by stretching it and kneading, following threads, circling around and coming back. I don't have a thought and fit language to it; I 'see' the words, and the words generate a meaning. This is why, in that same school English lesson, I could no more produce the required essay plan and follow it than I could fire a catapult to Mars. Everything starts from the seed of the word and out of that explode the streams of coloured bunting, like handkerchiefs from a magician's sleeve.

The late Mel Baggs, a mostly nonspeaking Autistic, writes:

> It took me quite a long time to develop the full understanding of there being pretty much one absolute (if broad) accepted use of language: to translate something about me into words so that someone else can translate those words into something about how they understand the world.[42]

Like Mel, I understand that in consensual reality this is what words are for, but I don't think I've ever accepted it. For me, words are like animals. They live a life of their own. I like to make them up and fineigle their meanings. It took a long time for me to realise that this is not what other people do. If a word sounds like a meaning, then to me it ought to be able to have that meaning. I don't care so much if I'm the only one who understands. I like that I have left a space in which your mind can turn, room for your own interpretation, for what *you* see.

I've learnt to edit myself. I've learnt to cover and remove. I've learnt to make the page look just grammatical enough, to change out the same word again, to weed out some of the pictures so as not to overwhelm. Still, a single word can be a way into a feeling or an understanding. It can be a book. It can shoot off meanings and meanings. It can look like a galaxy of different stars.

Afterword

The process of embodiment has always felt to me like following a string into the centre of the labyrinth – winding myself in. Often I have been travelling blind, but it didn't matter as long as I kept hold of the string. When I think of the innermost chamber, I see it walled like a nest with sticks and feathers, or drawn in charcoal with soft thick strokes of darkness. Now, in the second half of life, I am travelling backwards, releasing body to the waters and winds. There's a sense of rippling and flittering; dispersing and scattering: losing my pieces to all the shifting sands of the world, the kaleidoscopic patterns that dazzle and drift. I'm only just beginning to feel into this new becoming, the ravelling out.

Notes

AUTISM | A FLASH OF BRIGHTLY COLOURED FISH

1. 'Things That I Know Right Now', Wild Yoga blog, 10 March 2022: https://www.wildyoga.co.uk/2022/03/things-that-i-know-right-now.
2. The Autism Diagnostic Observation Schedule (ADOS) is an observation tool used to assess whether a person meets the criteria for a diagnosis of autism based on their presentation, behaviour and social responses.
3. The Office for Standards in Education, Children's Services and Skills – in other words, the UK schools inspectors.
4. Summerhill is a private British boarding school founded on the belief that the school should fit the child, not the other way around.
5. 'Access Intimacy, Interdependence and Disability Justice', Leaving Evidence blog, 12 April 2017: https://leavingevidence.wordpress.com/2017/04/12/access-intimacy-interdependence-and-disability-justice.
6. *The Tempest*, V, i, 269–70.
7. 'Outsider Artist Judith Scott': https://www.karmatube.org/videos.php?id=3563.
8. Temple Grandin and Richard Panek, *The Autistic Brain: Thinking Across the Spectrum*, Houghton Mifflin Harcourt, Boston and New York, 2013.
9. 'Temple Grandin on the Fukushima Nuclear Power Plant', Youtube, 24 March 2011: https://youtu.be/y8ABZ-qsEu8.
10. Sarah Schulman, *Empathy*, Penguin Books, 1992.
11. III, iii, 100–103. I don't think this is Shakespeare's intended meaning. It's probably more about hypocrisy. However, I like the alternative interpretation.
12. *Loud Hands: Autistic People Speaking*, The Autistic Self Advocacy Network, 2012.
13. Quoted on Emma's website in text now deleted.
14. Patti Smith, Bloomsbury Publishing, 2015.

15 Autistic.

16 A novel by Susanna Clark, Bloomsbury Publishing, 2020.

DANCE MOVEMENT | DEEP-WATER CONSCIOUSNESS

17 'Class Excerpts with Emilie Conrad: Feeling Sensation and More ...', Continuum Movement, Youtube, 19 December 2012: https://youtu.be/VXxDjAr_u0Y.

18 'Defining Neurodiversity', in *Neuroqueer Heresies: Notes on the Neurodiversity Paradigm, Autistic Empowerment, and Postnormal Possibilities*, Autonomous Press, Fort Worth TX, 2021.

19 *The Mind Tree: A Miraculous Child Breaks the Silence of Autism*, Tito Rajarshi Mukhopadhyay, Arcade Publishing, New York, 2000.

20 If you don't know what stimming is, you can find out here: Emma Fox, The Autisphere, 'Autism 101: What Is Stimming?' 3 September 2020: https://theautisphere.com/autism-101-what-is-stimming.

21 Autish has made a short video of Autistic women stim dancing. Find it in her blog post 'Stim Dance (#stopdropstim)': https://autish.wordpress.com/2020/02/08/stim-dance-stropdropstim.

22 *The Autistic Brain: Thinking Across the Spectrum*, Temple Grandin, Houghton Mifflin Harcourt Publishing Company, 2013.

ASHTANGA VINYASA | REPEAT AND RETURN

23 A way of engaging core body which is mostly the same as what we call 'pull-up' in ballet.

HYPERMOBILITY | TISSUE PAPER AND GLASS

24 To be honest, I've never really understood the explanation of 'zebra' as a term for people with a genetic hypermobility syndrome; however, if you're curious, you can find it in 'Why the Zebra?', Ehlers-Danlos Support UK: www.ehlers-danlos.org/about-us/charity-aims-and-focus/why-the-zebra.

25 And again, under the revised criteria, with 'hypermobile Ehlers-Danlos syndrome' (hEDS) in 2019.

26 This piece of writing is about a flare-up of Postural Orthostatic Tachycardia Syndrome (POTS).

27 One of the well-known senior ashtanga teachers.

TEACHING, FACILITATING, THERAPY | A WOMB, A LIMBECK

28 My bad. I should have asked before I booked. Today I would always do that.

29 'Disclosing one's Autistic identity, Annette Foster, with Chloe & Jessica: Aucademy in discussion', 16 November 2020: https://youtu.be/Sq82fb7NROY.

30 Aucademy, ' "Pathological" Demand Avoidance: Jodie Isitt educates Aucademy's Chloe and Tigger', 5 June 2021: https://youtu.be/ryWUrEoZgDY.

WRITING | STARBURST AND OCEAN

31 From Jess Glenny, 'Water', unpublished.

32 This attribution is controversial.

33 Leslie A. Marchand (ed), *Lord Byron: Selected Letters and Journals*, Harvard University Press, 1982.

34 *threads of yoga: a remix of patanjali-s sutra-s with commentary and reverie*, 2012.

35 Laurence Sterne, *The Life and Opinions of Tristram Shandy, Gentleman*, 1759–67. Virginia Woolf: it seems not. I thought I remembered a raindrop filling and filling in *The Waves*, but if it's there, I can't find the place. However, she uses 'fills and fills and fills' in 'Sketch of the Past': 'If life has a base that it stands upon, if it is a bowl that one fills and fills and fills – then my bowl without doubt stands upon this memory.' Perhaps it's all composted in my mind with words of my own.

36 Life on Land: *The Story of Continuum the World Renowned Self-discovery and Movement Method*, North Atlantic Books, 2007.

37 Myalgic encephalitis, now usually known as Chronic Fatigue Syndrome.

38 From *Stone Canoe: A journal of arts and ideas from upstate New York*, no. 2, spring 2008: https://www.ralphsavarese.com/writings/creative-nonfiction/the-lobes-of-autobiography. Ralph Savarese is a writer, academic, advocate for Autistic people and adoptive father of an Autistic son.

39 I emailed Ralph about this and he agreed.

40 Quoted in 'The Lobes of Autobiography'.

41 According to one study, the resting brains of Autistic children produce 42 per cent more information than those of non-autistic controls: Jeremy Dean, 'Intense World: Autistic Brains Create 42% More Information At Rest', PsyBlog, 5 February 2014: https://www.spring.org.uk/2014/02/intense-world-austistic-brains-create-42-more-information-at-rest.php.

42 'The Naked Mechanisms of Echolalia', Ballastexistenz blog, 5 April 2007: https://ballastexistenz.wordpress.com/2007/04/05/the-naked-mechanisms-of-echolalia.

Also by Jess Glenny

Hypermobility on the Yoga Mat

This book is an exploration of the neglected area of yoga and hypermobility. Hypermobile people are generally over-represented in yoga classes, yet often go unrecognised and receive little guidance about how to practise in hypermobility-friendly ways. Many yoga teachers have received little or no training about how to work with this vulnerable population.

This book considers what hypermobility is and offers teachers general guidelines as well as specific practical techniques for including hypermobile students safely and effectively in classes. For hypermobile students themselves there are lots of suggestions for making a yoga practice helpful and beneficial.

Also including information about co-existing conditions, the intersection of hypermobility and neurodiversity, and much more, *Hypermobility on the Yoga Mat* is the go-to resource for both hypermobile yoga practitioners and yoga teachers encountering hypermobile students.

The Yoga Teacher Mentor

How do we generate enlivening relationships with our students? Create welcoming and inclusive spaces? Navigate common ethical issues? Remain inspired as we encounter the routine challenges of teaching yoga day-to-day? Full of practical information for new teachers, this book is much more than a beginner's guide, considering questions that continue to arise through the course of a teaching life.

With reflective and experiential exercises throughout, the book is designed to create different lenses through which teachers of all stripes and vintages can view difficult situations and amplify their understanding of what it means to hold rich and meaningful classes. The intention is to invite self-reflection and offer possibilities, without being prescriptive. Emphasising the need for yoga teachers to know about more than alignment and sequencing, *The Yoga Teacher Mentor* accompanies the reader through the rich, complex and rewarding process of teaching yoga.

Printed in Great Britain
by Amazon